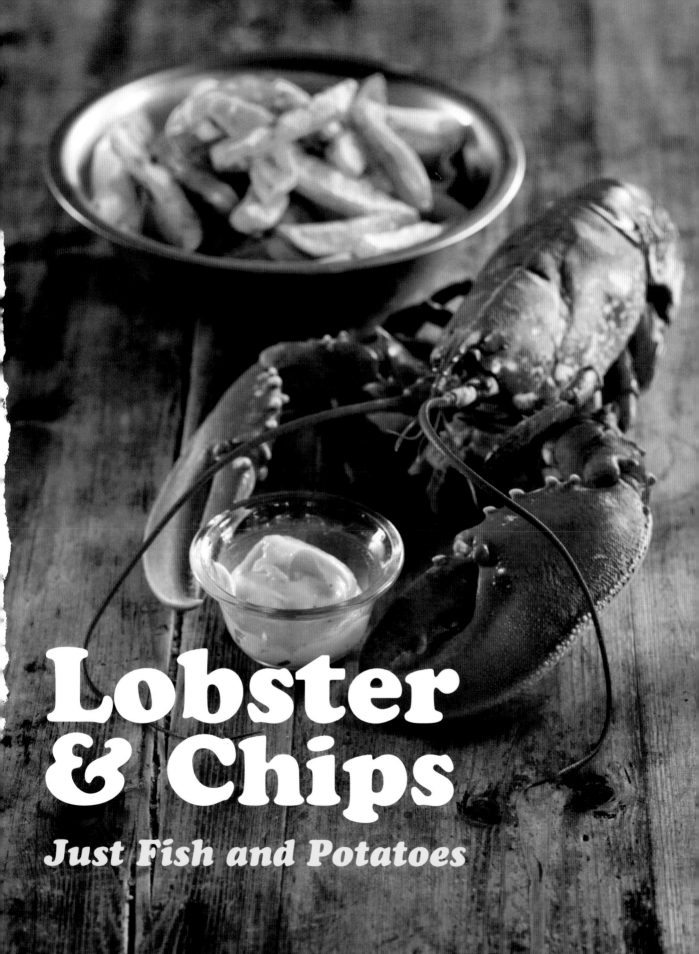

Lobster & Chips

Just Fish and Potatoes

FOR MY PARENTS, KEVIN AND JOAN,
MY SIBLINGS, JOANNE, KATHY, TINA, BRENDAN AND CLAIRE,
AND ESPECIALLY DAVID.

Lobster & Chips

Just Fish and Potatoes

A.

ABSOLUTE PRESS

TRISH HILFERTY

PHOTOGRAPHY BY JASON LOWE

First published in Great Britain in 2005 by
Absolute Press
Scarborough House
29 James Street West
Bath BA1 2BT
Phone 44 (0) 1225 316013
Fax 44 (0) 1225 445836
E-mail info@absolutepress.co.uk
Website www.absolutepress.co.uk

Publisher Jon Croft
Commissioning Editor Meg Avent
Editor Jane Middleton
Designer Matt Inwood
Publishing Assistant Meg Devenish

Photography © Jason Lowe

A catalogue record of this book is available from
the British Library

ISBN 1 904573 28 2

Printed and bound by Butler and Tanner, Frome,
Somerset

CONTENTS

NOTE FOR AMERICAN READERS

In the recipes, American measures are given in brackets after the metric measures.
Below are the American terms for some of the ingredients and equipment used in this book:

baking sheet = cookie sheet
bicarbonate of soda = baking soda
black pudding = blood sausage
chips = French fries
cling film = plastic wrap
coriander = cilantro (when referring to the green, leafy herb rather than the seeds)
crisps = potato chips
double cream = heavy cream
dried yeast = active dry yeast
Easyblend yeast = dry yeast that is added directly to the flour; if unavailable, use ordinary dry yeast and mix it with water in the usual way
fish slice = slotted spatula
fresh yeast = compressed yeast
frying pan = skillet
greaseproof paper = parchment paper
Greek yoghurt = thick plain yoghurt
grey mullet = mullet, striped bass
grilled = broiled

lemon sole = English sole, flounder
ling = lingcod, cusk
loaf tin = loaf pan
monkfish = anglerfish
natural yoghurt = plain yoghurt
pepper, red or green = bell pepper, red or green
plaice = flounder, sole
plain flour = all-purpose flour
prawns = shrimp
red mullet = goatfish
rocket = arugula
sea bream = snapper
sea trout = steelhead trout
self-raising flour = self-rising flour
sieve = strainer
single cream = light cream
spring onion = green onion
strong flour = bread flour
tomato purée = tomato paste

INTRODUCTION

I can't remember a time in my life when I haven't been fanatical about food. Many of my earliest memories are linked to cooking and eating. Whether these are of trawling around markets with my mother while she shopped for dinner, fighting with my siblings over who could get into the kitchen first to make cakes at the weekend, or helping my dad stoke the barbie, I was always in the thick of it.

I always wanted to cook, and now that I've been doing just that professionally for 20 years there are many lessons that I've learned. The first and arguably the most important is to begin with the best ingredients. I value simplicity and good provenance, so whether I'm cooking at home or in the pub I always use the best produce I can get my hands on. Shopping wisely is the beginning of any good meal, and by preparing good ingredients simply you can be sure that they will shine.

Two ingredients that are a constant on my menus are fish and potatoes. Besides making up Britain's national dish, fish and chips, they are tasty, healthy and incredibly versatile. Perfectly happy to sit together on a plate or to be the star of their own show, they offer something for every occasion, be it a light lunch, a posh dinner party or an easy snack.

Fish and potatoes are a universal pairing, and dedicating a whole book to the subject has let me explore the myriad ways of combining two of the world's best-loved ingredients. I grew up in Sydney, a city on the sea, where fish played an important part in our mealtimes – from fish-and-chip dinners after a day on the beach, to Friday-night suppers of my mother's delicious fishcakes or the fish pie my grandmother made, using a recipe adapted from her English mother. The cultural diversity of a big city also gave me an insight into other cuisines. There were large Greek, Italian and Asian communities where we lived, and an appreciation of seafood was essential to their cooking. So I learned the difference between good home-made taramasalata and shop-bought tubs, and discovered Thai fish curries, stuffed squid and braised octopus. After this, travelling was the natural next step for me. I discovered the food of northern Europe, the Americas and North Africa, all of whom have their own unique ways of combining fish and potatoes.

This book is a collection of some of my favourite recipes, which I've cooked both professionally and at home. However, I'm a firm believer that some recipes, like rules, are made to be broken, so please feel free to adapt and experiment. As long as you always remember to use the freshest ingredients, you won't be disappointed.

TRISH HILFERTY, AUGUST 2005

ACKNOWLEDGEMENTS

For making this book happen, I must first thank David Tatham, Tom Norrington-Davies and Jason Lowe; their good advice and encouragement kept me on track – extra thanks to Jason for his beautiful photography. Then Jon, Meg and Matt at Absolute for giving me such an opportunity and Jane Middleton for making sense of it all.

Many thanks to the following:
Mike Belben for unflagging support;
Sam Waterhouse, Jorge Cardoso, Sath Pahlath, Ed Nassau-Lake and all the staff at the Fox, past and present; Ben Woodcraft; Julian Birch; Charlie Hicks; Wendy Sayell; Jonathon Jones; Harry Lester; Adam Robinson; Paul and Terry Bailey at Lenards; Pat and Peter Tatham.

BUYING FISH

Fish and shellfish must be truly fresh to be outstanding. There is nothing that you can do to disguise the flavour of an old, tired fish. Sure, you could wash the fillets under the tap or squeeze lemon over them but they will never taste sensational, and they should. Why compromise on flavour?

Choosing the best and freshest fish isn't as difficult as some people think. My first piece of advice is to follow your gut instinct: if a fish looks good and healthy, it will most likely taste good, too. Very fresh fish should not smell fishy, it should just have a faint aroma of the sea – anything stronger and it's probably been on the slab a little too long. The eyes should be clear and bright, not dull, and they should protrude slightly from the head. The body should be firm and bouncy when you press the skin and, if the fish has scales, they should be shiny and tight. Probably the most important point is to check the gills. They should be a bright rosy red, with no hint of brown, and shouldn't be covered in a gooey film of mucus.

Armed with this knowledge, it's best to buy whole fish, even if you only need fillets. Ask your fishmonger to fillet it for you, then you can take the bones and trimmings home and with them **make this stock**: simply put them in a pan with enough water to cover, plus chopped onion, leek, celery, a bay leaf and a sprig of thyme, simmer for 30 minutes, then strain.

If you have to buy fish ready filleted, avoid soggy or discoloured fillets. They may have been previously frozen and will never have the flavour of really fresh fish. Choose fillets or fish steaks that are firm and neatly trimmed, with translucent flesh. If you can't get the fish you want, a good strategy is to buy the best-looking fish in the shop and adapt your recipe to suit. An experienced fishmonger will be able to advise you on this.

If you are buying smoked fish, it should have an agreeable smoky aroma and the flesh should be firm, with a glossy appearance. Don't buy smoked fish that is sticky or slimy and try to avoid dyed fish. Instead choose naturally smoked fish, which has a paler colour and hasn't been treated with any nasty chemicals.

Squid, cuttlefish and octopus should smell sweet and have shiny skin and firm flesh. Try to buy them with their guts intact – a sure sign that they haven't been previously frozen and are therefore genuinely fresh. They are easily cleaned. I've given instructions with their recipes in this book, though a fishmonger will always do this for you if necessary.

When choosing shellfish, make sure their shells are intact and not cracked or broken. Oysters, mussels and clams should be tightly shut, though open mussels and clams are acceptable if they shut swiftly when tapped. Throw away any that don't.

It's still difficult to buy fresh prawns in this country, though they are becoming increasingly available in the summer months. Luckily, the most readily available frozen prawns are caught in the North Atlantic and snap frozen at sea. They are usually an excellent product.

I prefer to buy 'green' or raw prawns rather than cooked, as they take on the flavours of the seasonings they are cooked with. When buying these prawns in their shells, make sure they have a good bright colour and smell of the sea. Look out for any black discoloration around the head and legs, which means they're on their way out.

Crabs and lobsters are best bought alive. Look for a beast that's still active. They will stay alive in the fridge for two or three days covered with damp newspaper or a cloth. The most humane way to dispatch them is to pop them into the freezer for a couple of hours to send them off to sleep before boiling.

Good cooked crabs and lobsters feel heavy for their size – that way you know they're full of meat. They shouldn't have any liquid sloshing around inside the body, which means the flesh is deteriorating.

When shopping for fish and shellfish, my first stop would always be my local fishmonger's. Besides having a larger variety on offer than a supermarket, fishmonger's shops give you the opportunity to have a good look at the quality of the fish before you buy. At first the wide variety can be bewildering but it's worth learning a little about the different types of fish – oily, meaty, flat, round – as this can help you understand the best way to handle them.

Unfortunately not everyone has access to a fishmonger's, in which case the supermarket probably seems like the only option. Much supermarket fish is pre-packaged, though some of the larger stores do have a dedicated fish counter selling fillets or steaks of 'speciality fish', such as tuna, skate and trout, alongside shellfish such as dressed crabs, lobsters and mussels.

However, if you want really fresh fish an increasingly viable option is mail order. You can find a great many companies trading this way via the internet. Most of them sell direct from coastal towns and send their fish overnight, packaged in polystyrene boxes, guaranteeing the freshness a supermarket can't.

It's always best to buy your fish on the day that you want to eat it – certainly no more than 24 hours in advance. Take it straight home and refrigerate it as soon as possible. I always remove my purchase from the wrapping, lay it flat on a plate (skin-side up, if filleted) and cover it with cling film before putting it in the coldest part of the fridge. If you do find yourself with extra fish or simply can't get around to cooking it straight away, you can freeze it successfully. Wrap the fish tightly in cling film or put it in a freezer bag, making sure there is no air trapped inside, then label and date the package. Be sure to use it within two weeks, defrosting it slowly in the fridge on a layer of kitchen paper.

The basic rule is that meaty, firm-fleshed fish such as halibut or monkfish freezes better than soft, delicate fish, such as plaice or sole, or oily-fleshed fish, such as mackerel or herring. Smoked fish freezes well but I find that once defrosted it is best used in soups or kedgeree, as the texture is affected by the freezing process. Squid, cuttlefish and octopus are the most successful varieties for freezing. The texture of the flesh slowly breaks down, making it more tender.

You may notice that there are a lot of recipes for salt cod in this book – that's because I'm its biggest fan. Salt cod comes in different forms, depending on where you search for it. In a quality deli you may find a whole side of salted cod, perfect poached with aioli. Be sure to use the head end – a fine piece of meaty fish – for this, and then use the tail end for brandade, fishcakes or stews. At the other end of the spectrum are the rectangular packets of salt cod available in Jamaican or African stores – perfect, of course, with ackee (see page 133). Remember that salt cod dishes need a little forward planning, as the fish has to be soaked in fresh water overnight to leach out the salt.

You could always salt your own fish. Besides cod, I salt hake, coley and pollock, which all take to the curing process perfectly. Lay a kilo of fish fillets skin-side up in a dish and sprinkle over enough fine sea salt to coat them in a loose blanket. Cover and leave overnight in the fridge. At this point the fish will need only a quick soak – say, around half an hour – before you use it. It will keep, well covered in salt, for at least a month in the fridge, as the salt draws all the liquid from it, turning it into brine and effectively curing the fish. Don't be tempted to drain off this liquid as it protects the fish. The longer it's been salted, the longer you will need to soak it before cooking – at least overnight in several changes of water.

SUSTAINABLE FISH

Over the last 30 years the demand for fish and shellfish has doubled. So how do we continue to eat the fish we love while protecting the once-plentiful stocks from dying out?

While there is no doubt that some species in our coastal waters are in danger, there are still a number of stocks that remain healthy – the ones that come from well-managed and sustainable sources. So the best thing we can do for dwindling fish stocks and the environment is to shop responsibly. This means avoiding fish caught deep at sea in factory ships. Most of these deep-sea fish are captured in nets up to a mile wide, by ships that, with the aid of global positioning systems and sonar, can identify whole shoals and scoop them up into their purse-shaped nets, then pump them into their hold and leave when the holds are full – inevitably taking a percentage of rare and endangered species along with their intended catch. These fish are likely to be at least five or six days' old by the time they get to a fishmonger's. Deepwater fish are also thought to live longer, are slower to mature and breed and, as a result, are always in danger of overfishing.

What we should be buying instead are seasonal, inshore fish, line-caught in day boats. The fishermen who man single-trip boats go out to sea for short periods of around 12 hours and as a result come back to port with the freshest fish. Their movements are restricted by the weather and the seasons, they specifically target the fish running at the time, catch fish of the right size and stick to quotas. Besides the freshness of their catch and the fact that they don't literally vacuum up the sea beds, another very good reason to favour them is that they are independent and support whole communities, employing local deckhands, boat builders, mechanics and so on. A good fishmonger will be able to tell you how his or her fish were caught.

We should also try to be adventurous in the varieties of fish we choose, to avoid putting too much pressure on traditional species. So instead of always going for cod or haddock, which together account for 30 per cent of the total British fish consumption, look for something different, such as pollock and whiting, both members of the cod family, with sweet, firm white flesh. Websites such as www.fishonline.org, or the Marine Conservation Society's website, www.mcsuk.org, carry up-to-the-minute information on sustainable fish stocks and provide lists of which fish to buy and which to avoid.

The legacy of overfishing has led to an increase in fish farming, which accounts for a large proportion of fish sold today. Yet, just as with conventional farming, not all fish farms are ethical or responsible. Some, though by no means all, treat their fish like battery-farmed chickens, stuffing them into cages and feeding them on growth hormones, dyes and pesticides, which then leach into the surrounding waters and play havoc with the eco-system.

The best farmed fish is certified organic, to Soil Association standards (www.soilassociation.org). Organically farmed fish are grown in natural conditions – free range, if you like. They are bred in cages out at sea that are not heavily stocked, giving them ample room to move around. The strong tidal currents ensure the fish get plenty of exercise, which makes them stronger and more robust. This results in firmer flesh and a much better flavour. Most importantly, they are fed on pellets made from the by-products of fish caught for human consumption, not nasty industrial fishmeal. At the time of writing, the most widely available organic fish on our high streets are salmon and trout, though cod, sea bass and halibut are now being organically reared and do make an appearance in good fishmonger's shops.

So, if you want to shop ethically for fish, always be sure to ask where and how the fish you buy was caught. If you can find line-caught, this is the way to go. Otherwise stick to organically farmed varieties, some of which are available in good supermarkets (those that still bother to have a fish counter). And don't be afraid to try something different – you might be pleasantly surprised.

BUYING POTATOES
BY CHARLIE HICKS

Every food culture has its favourite carbohydrate – a starchy bulking agent to stretch more expensive ingredients and provide energy. Noodles, rice, pasta and corn are all acceptable in their own way, but for sheer versatility and deliciousness nothing beats the potato. Hot chips sprinkled with malt vinegar; a mound of creamy mash; spuds roasted in duck fat; the creamy, melting flesh of a boiled new potato. Polenta doesn't really get a look in, does it?

For me, new potatoes start with the first outdoor Jersey Royals, which usually arrive in late April or early May. These are swiftly followed by new potatoes from Cornwall, and then from the rest of the country. It's always best to buy local. Nothing beats the taste of a just-dug spud, so the closer to home, the better. All new potatoes have a loose skin, which you can push off with your thumb. Once the skin has tightened, they are no longer new. The little potatoes, or 'Mids' to the trade, that pass themselves off as new throughout the rest of the year are really no such thing. They used to be graded out and used for animal food or thrown away, until unscrupulous wholesalers and growers realised that they could command a premium price if they were washed, prettily packaged and sold to the catering trade as 'new potatoes'.

Larger, main-crop potatoes begin with First Earlies in late July and early August. Most main-crop potatoes will have been lifted by the end of the autumn, when many of them are put into store to keep us supplied for the rest of the year. Main-crop potatoes store well (although new ones don't) but gradually their starch turns to sugar and, after about five or six months, the quality really begins to decline. Fortunately this coincides with new-crop potatoes coming in from southern Europe. A particular favourite is the Cyprus spud, with its long oval shape and distinctive orange skin stained by the soil. There are also some very good new potatoes from Egypt, Majorca and, more recently, Spain. These should see you through the lean times until the first Jerseys come round again.

Besides new and main-crop, potatoes are also divided into two rather loose groups: floury (sometimes called mealy) and waxy. Most potatoes grown in the UK are floury varieties. These are low in moisture, contain more starch and tend to crumble easily when cooked. They bake and mash very well and produce the best chips and a crisper roast potato. Potatoes from the rest of Europe are usually waxy, the denser flesh holding together rather better. Waxy potatoes have a high water content and lower starch, and tend to keep their shape when boiling. This makes them ideal for salads and sautés. Most new potatoes are waxy ones.

All the recipes in this book specify either waxy or floury potatoes. Because they serve different purposes, it's important to be able to distinguish between the two. Having said that, not all potatoes behave exactly as they should. A spud that mashes beautifully in one kitchen will produce a sullen, gluey mess just down the road. One cook's marvellous chipper will be a sticky, caramelised disaster for another. To complicate matters still further, some chefs like to break the rules – often with very successful results. I remember Trish telling me once that she was using Spunta, a yellow-fleshed, waxy variety, for mash. Sacrilege! Spunta are for chips, everyone knows that. Even so, I took a few home and tried them out. She was absolutely right: they produced a magnificent mash, rich, smooth and creamy, with a beautiful, deep yellow colour. That taught me.

So the best advice? Try every spud you can lay your hands on till you find out what works for you. Overleaf is a guide to the better-known varieties.

POTATO VARIETIES

There are hundreds of different types of potato grown in the UK but only a very small percentage of these are grown commercially, and even fewer are available on the high street or in the supermarket. Generally, what we see in the shops are the more popular main-crop types, such as King Edward, Desireé and Maris Piper, and often-nameless new potatoes.

FLOURY POTATOES

Maris Piper The most popular variety, this has pale skin and creamy white flesh. A good all-rounder.

King Edward A long, oval shape with pale flesh and cream-coloured skin with pink blotches. A good masher, it makes wonderful roasties and chips.

Cara A round potato with pale skin and pink eyes. The perfect baking potato.

Golden Wonder Pale skin and flesh. Excellent for roasting.

Kerrs Pink Great for roasts and chips but it tends to get a little waterlogged when boiled, so avoid this one for mash.

Romano A short, oval potato with red skin. Bake, roast or chip.

WAXY POTATOES

Desireé A large, oval potato with red skin and yellow flesh. Good for chips and roasting but not so good for mash.

Ulster Prince A small, oval potato with white skin and flesh, this makes a good addition to stews or warm salads.

Marfona A short, yellow-skinned potato with pale yellow flesh. It makes a fabulous roast potato cooked from raw, with lots of olive oil, sea salt and rosemary.

Estima Yellow skin and flesh. Great for boiling, baking and roasting.

Spunta A large, oval potato with creamy skin and yellow flesh. A great all-rounder and, contrary to received potato wisdom, these waxy spuds make lovely mash.

Cyprus A large orange-skinned potato, good for baking, boiling, chipping or roasting.

NEW POTATOES

Jersey Royals The first and best of the new potatoes, these should simply be boiled and tossed with a knob of butter and some chopped parsley.

Cornish Almost as good as Jerseys, these should be treated in the same way.

Roseval Red skinned with pale yellow flesh. This French variety boils well and makes great potato salads.

Nicola Yellow skin and flesh. Good for boiling and salads.

Pink Fir Apple Pink-skinned with knobbly flesh, these are great for salads. They also boil and roast very well.

Charlotte, La Ratte, Belle de Fontenay Three more French varieties with firm, yellow flesh. Good all-rounders and particularly good salad potatoes.

SWEET POTATOES

Native to South America and the West Indies, sweet potatoes are not related to potatoes but can be prepared in exactly the same way. They particularly suit boiling, baking, mashing and deep-frying. Their pink skin conceals either white or orange flesh. The orange-fleshed ones are generally sweeter and less mealy, so go for these if possible (often the only way to find out what you're getting is surreptitiously to scrape off a little skin with your fingernail).

SOUPS

SIMPLE FISHY BROTH WITH GNOCCHI

This is the simplest fish soup I know. It doesn't have a long list of ingredients or a convoluted method, it doesn't even need fish stock, though it will benefit from it if you have any to hand. Since it uses only one type of fish, it has a clean and singular flavour, which makes the perfect vehicle for potato gnocchi (see page 147). I prefer to use red mullet, though any white-fleshed fish such as halibut, sea bream or hake will do beautifully.

3 tablespoons olive oil
1 onion, chopped
1 fennel bulb, chopped
2 garlic cloves, chopped
400g (14 ounces) tomatoes, skinned and
  chopped, or canned tomatoes, drained
A strip of orange zest
A pinch of saffron threads
1 bay leaf
500g (1 pound 2 ounces) fish fillets, skinned
  and cut into 1cm ($^1/_2$ inch) dice
1.5 litres ($6^1/_4$ cups) water (or fish stock
  – see p9)
1 quantity of Potato Gnocchi (see page 147)
Sea salt and freshly ground black pepper

Heat the olive oil in a heavy-based pan, add the onion, fennel and garlic and sauté for 5 minutes, stirring occasionally. Add the tomatoes, orange zest, saffron and bay leaf and simmer for 5 minutes. Now add the fish, season with sea salt and pepper and pour in the water. Bring to the boil and simmer for about 20 minutes, until everything is tender. Remove from the heat and leave to cool slightly. Discard the bay leaf and orange zest, then purée the soup in a blender. Pour the soup into a clean pan, add the cooked gnocchi, warm through and adjust the seasoning. Ladle into warmed soup bowls and serve straight away.

Serves 6

OYSTER, POTATO AND WATERCRESS SOUP

Watercress and shellfish go together beautifully. A striking bright green in colour, this is a soothing soup made ever so slightly decadent by the salty tang of the oysters. It is very good with watercress sandwiches, made by mixing chopped watercress with softened butter and sandwiching it between slices of fresh white bread. Remove the crusts and cut the sandwiches into triangles.

60g (4 tablespoons) unsalted butter
2 onions, chopped
*1kg (2¼ pounds) floury potatoes, peeled
 and diced*
500ml (2 cups) milk
1 litre (4 cups) water or light chicken stock
*2 bunches of watercress, tough stalks
 removed*
6–12 oysters – it's up to you
Sea salt and freshly ground black pepper

Melt the butter in a large pan and add the onions. Cover and cook over a low heat until the onions are soft, stirring occasionally. Add the potatoes, then the milk and water or stock. Bring to a simmer and cook until the potatoes are soft. Add the watercress and cook for another minute.

Liquidise the soup in a blender and then return it to the pan. Reheat gently and season to taste. Place 1 or 2 oysters in the bottom of each soup bowl and ladle over the hot soup to poach the oysters slightly.

Serves 6

CALDEIRADA

Portugal's caldeirada is more of a big fish stew than a soup. This version is from the book, *Big Flavours and Rough Edges* (Headline, 2001), written by the staff of the Eagle pub in London's Farringdon Road. Jorge Cardoso, a chef at the Eagle and a native of Lisbon, used to take great pleasure in making this most weekends. A popular dish, it very rarely lasted until the end of lunch.

18 raw king prawns
About 40 large mussels
2 onions, finely chopped
3 garlic cloves, finely chopped
4 tablespoons olive oil
2 bay leaves
A pinch of saffron strands
2 green and 2 red peppers, cut into strips
3 large waxy potatoes, peeled and chopped
*400g (14 ounces) canned peeled plum
    tomatoes, drained and chopped*
1 tablespoon tomato purée
A pinch of hot paprika
100ml (scant 1/2 cup) white wine
*500g (1 pound 2 ounces) monkfish tail,
    cut into discs 2cm (3/4 inch) thick*
*500g (1 pound 2 ounces) sea bass or bream
    fillets, cut into 3cm (1 1/4 inch) pieces*
*500g (1 pound 2 ounces) mackerel or sardine
    fillets, cut into 3cm (1 1/4 inch) pieces*
Lemon halves, to serve
Sea salt and freshly ground black pepper

For the stock
1 celery stalk, chopped
1 carrot, chopped
1 garlic clove, chopped
1 bay leaf
3 black peppercorns
1 litre (4 cups) water

Pull the heads off the prawns, then peel off the shells. Set aside the heads and shells. Use the tip of a sharp knife to remove the black intestinal vein from the back of each prawn – the prawn's last meal. Put the heads and shells in a pan with all the stock ingredients and bring to the boil. Lower the heat to a simmer and cook for 45 minutes, skimming off any scum with a ladle. Strain the stock through a sieve and set aside.

Scrub the mussels to remove any sand or barnacles and pull out their beards – the hairy bit poking out of the shell. Tap any open mussels on the work surface to see if they close; if they don't, be sure to discard them, to eliminate the risk of upset stomachs. Set the mussels aside.

In a large saucepan, gently fry the onions and garlic in the olive oil until soft and translucent. Add the bay leaves and saffron and fry until the onions are light brown. Add the peppers and potatoes and fry for 3 minutes, then stir in the tomatoes and cook for a further 3 minutes. Add the hot stock, tomato purée, paprika and wine. Bring to the boil, reduce the heat to medium and cook until the potatoes are almost tender; they should still be a little hard.

Raise the heat and add the monkfish and prawns; 2 minutes later, add the bass or bream and mussels. After a further 2 minutes, add the mackerel or sardines and turn off the heat. Season to taste. The mackerel or sardines will cook in the residual heat.

Serve in large bowls with a squeeze of lemon to add freshness and acidity.

Serves 8-10

CULLEN SKINK

The intriguingly named Cullen Skink is a rich, creamy soup to savour on a cold night in front of a roaring fire. The recipe is originally from the small fishing village of Cullen, on the Moray Firth in Scotland, and uses the local speciality, Finnan haddock (or haddie, as it is known there) – haddock that have been split, with the central bone left in, then cold-smoked over wood. If you can't get hold of haddie, use undyed smoked haddock.

*500g (1 pound 2 ounces) Finnan haddock
or undyed smoked haddock
About 600ml (2^1/$_2$ cups) milk
15g (1 tablespoon) unsalted butter
1 onion, sliced
225g (8 ounces) floury potatoes, peeled,
diced and rinsed (this removes excess
starch)
600ml (2^1/$_2$ cups) water
100ml (scant ^{1}/$_2$ cup) single cream
2 tablespoons chopped chives
Sea salt and freshly ground black pepper*

Put the haddock in a pan and add the milk; it should just cover the fish. Bring to the boil, turn down to a simmer and cook for 5 minutes, then set aside.

Melt the butter in a separate pan, add the onion and sweat over a low heat until it is soft and translucent. Add the potatoes and water, bring to the boil and simmer until the potatoes are almost cooked.

Remove the fish from the milk. Pour the milk through a sieve into the pan with the potatoes and cook for 5 minutes.

Meanwhile, flake the fish, discarding the skin and bones.

I prefer a chunky texture, so it is best to crush the potatoes gently with a fork or potato masher. Finally add the flaked fish and the cream and simmer for 5 minutes. Pour into warm bowls and scatter with the chopped chives.

Serves 6-8

SALT COD, LEEK AND PORCINI BROTH

A winter warmer with a rich Italian flavour. The intensity of the dried porcini mushrooms makes them the perfect base to use in soups. You can buy them ready sliced in little bags in delis or supermarkets.

Besides the porcini, this broth employs the powerful flavour of salt cod. Despite these two massive flavours, the saltiness of the fish combines really well with the earthy taste of the mushrooms.

25g (1 cup) dried porcini mushrooms
50g (3¹/₂ tablespoons) unsalted butter
500g (1 pound 2 ounces) leeks, sliced
2 garlic cloves, chopped
2 bay leaves
1kg (2¹/₄ pounds) floury potatoes, peeled,
  cut into 4cm (1¹/₂ inch) chunks and rinsed
  (this removes excess starch, which could
  make the soup thick and gluey)
250g (9 ounces) salt cod, soaked for 12 hours
  or overnight in several changes of water
2 tablespoons chopped chives
Sea salt and freshly ground black pepper

Pour 200ml (scant 1 cup) warm water over the porcini and leave to soak for 10 minutes. Drain the mushrooms, reserving the soaking liquid, and squeeze out excess water.

Melt the butter in a pan and add the leeks, garlic and bay leaves, plus a pinch of salt. Add the porcini, then cover and cook over a low heat until the leeks and mushrooms are soft. Add the potatoes to the pan and pour in the reserved porcini liquor plus enough cold water to cover. Bring to the boil and simmer until the potatoes are tender.

Drain the salt cod and cut it into thin strips. Add these to the pan and simmer for 2–3 minutes; the fish will turn opaque when it is done. Season with sea salt and black pepper. Ladle the soup into bowls and scatter with the chives.

Serves 6

NEW ENGLAND CLAM CHOWDER

The chowder is a staple of the northeast coast of America, though each state has a slightly different version. The name comes from the French word *chaudron*, a large pot in which fishermen would stew surplus fish. From France, the chowder travelled to Canada and made its way down the coastline, becoming the popular American dish it is today.

This recipe and the two that follow come from New England, Manhattan and Canada respectively and each has its own distinctive character. An ingredient that is traditional in all American chowders, however, is the cracker, broken up over the top or sometimes crushed in the bottom of the bowl to thicken the soup. You can do this if you like, though I prefer it without.

If you think of chowder today, it is the New England recipe that usually comes to mind. Cooked with milk or cream (or both), it is based on the milk and fish stews of the French Atlantic coast.

1kg (2¼ pounds) clams
1 litre (4 cups) fish stock or water
30g (2 tablespoons) unsalted butter
200g (7 ounces) smoked streaky bacon, diced
1 onion, diced
A bay leaf
500g (1 pound 2 ounces) floury potatoes,
   peeled and diced
250ml (1 cup) milk
250ml (1 cup) double cream
2 tablespoons chopped chives or parsley
Sea salt and freshly ground black pepper

Wash the clams under cold running water to remove grit or sand, discarding any open ones that don't close when tapped on the work surface. Place them in a large pan with 250ml (1 cup) of the stock or water, cover and bring to the boil. The steam will open the clams after 3–5 minutes. When they are cool enough to handle, remove the clams from their shells and set aside. Strain the cooking liquid through a fine sieve, as it may contain a little sand. Pour the cooking liquid over the clams to prevent them drying out.

Melt the butter in a large pan, add the bacon and sauté until golden brown. Add the onion and bay leaf, then cover and cook for about 5 minutes, until the onion is soft.

Then add the remaining stock or water and the potatoes and bring to the boil. Reduce the heat to medium and simmer for 10 minutes. Add the milk and cream and simmer for a further 10 minutes, until the potatoes are tender. At this point you can crush the potatoes a little with a potato masher or fork to thicken the soup slightly, if you like. Add the clams and their cooking liquor and heat through gently, then season to taste. Ladle the soup into warm bowls, sprinkle with the chopped chives or parsley and serve.

Serves 6-8

MANHATTAN CLAM CHOWDER

Unlike the New England version, the Manhattan chowder uses tomatoes in the base. It was adapted by New York's large Italian immigrant population, who came mostly from the south of Italy and were unaccustomed to a diet rich in cream.

1kg (2¹/₄ pounds) clams
125ml (¹/₂ cup) white wine
30g (2 tablespoons) unsalted butter
200g (7 ounces) smoked streaky bacon, diced
1 onion, diced
2 celery sticks, diced
1 carrot, diced
400g (14 ounces) tomatoes, skinned and
*   chopped, or canned chopped tomatoes*
500g (1 pound 2 ounces) floury potatoes,
*   peeled and diced*
1 litre (4 cups) water
3 tablespoons chopped parsley
Sea salt and freshly ground black pepper

Wash the clams under cold running water to remove grit or sand, discarding any open ones that don't close when tapped on the work surface. Put the clams in a large pan with the white wine, cover and bring to the boil. The steam will open the clams in about 3–5 minutes. When they are cool enough to handle, remove the clams from their shells and set aside. Strain the cooking liquid through a fine sieve, as it may contain a little sand. Pour the cooking liquid over the clams to prevent them drying out.

Melt the butter in a large pan, add the bacon and sauté until golden brown.
Add the onion, celery and carrot, then cover and cook gently for 5 minutes, until softened. Add the tomatoes, potatoes, water and 2 tablespoons of the parsley. Bring to the boil, then reduce the heat and simmer for about 20 minutes, until the potatoes are tender. Add the clams and their cooking liquor and heat through gently, then season to taste. Ladle the soup into warm bowls and scatter with the remaining parsley.

Serves 6-8

SCALLOP CHOWDER

This is an adaptation of a recipe from Nova Scotia, the main area for scallop fishing in Canada, where the early French settlers heavily influenced the cuisine.

50g (3^1/$_2$ tablespoons) salted butter
200g (7 ounces) smoked streaky bacon, diced
1 onion, diced
2 celery stalks, diced
30g (3^1/$_2$ tablespoons) plain flour
1.25 litres (5 cups) milk
A bay leaf
500g (1 pound 2 ounces) floury potatoes,
    peeled and diced
12 large scallops or 24 small queen scallops,
    cut into 2cm (^{3}/$_4$ inch) dice
Lemon juice, to taste
2 tablespoons chopped chives
Sea salt and freshly ground black pepper

Melt the butter in a pan, add the bacon and sauté until it is golden brown. Add the onion and celery, cover and cook gently for about 5 minutes, until softened. Now add the flour and stir until you have a paste (a roux); this will thicken the soup. Gradually stir in the milk, then add the bay leaf and potatoes and bring to a simmer. Don't let it boil vigorously or it may curdle. Cook for about 20 minutes, until the potatoes are tender. Add the scallops to the pan and poach lightly for about 1 minute, until they look opaque. Season with salt and black pepper, plus a squeeze of lemon juice to taste. Ladle into warm soup bowls and sprinkle with the chives.

Serves 6-8

SEA BASS, SAFFRON AND POTATO BROTH

This recipe is a kind of deconstructed fish soup, based on the great soup-plus-fish dishes of the Mediterranean coast of France, such as bouillabaisse and bourride. Like most Provençal soups, it makes a substantial meal with toast, aioli and a salad on the side.

600g (1¼ pounds) Bintje or Roseval
  potatoes, peeled and cut into slices 2cm
  (¾ inch) thick
6 x 120g (4-ounce) sea bass fillets
A little olive oil for frying
Lemon juice, to taste
Sea salt and freshly ground black pepper
Aioli (see page 152), to serve

For the broth
1 tablespoon olive oil
1 onion, chopped
2 garlic cloves, crushed
1 fennel bulb, chopped
2 celery stalks, chopped
A pinch of saffron threads
1 teaspoon fennel seeds
1 teaspoon coriander seeds
100ml (scant ½ cup) white wine
750ml (3 cups) fish stock
200g (7 ounces) tomatoes, skinned
  and chopped
½ small red chilli, seeded and chopped

To make the broth, heat the olive oil in a pan, add the onion and garlic with a pinch of sea salt and cook gently until the onion is soft. Add the fennel, celery, saffron and the seeds, then cover and cook over a low heat for 5 minutes. Pour in the wine and simmer until it has reduced by half. Add the stock, tomatoes and chilli, bring to the boil, then turn down to a simmer. Cook for 30 minutes or until the vegetables are soft. Allow the broth to cool a little, then purée it in a blender and return to the pan to keep warm. Cook the potatoes in boiling salted water until tender, then drain and set aside.

Season the sea bass fillets with salt and pepper. Heat a little olive oil in a large frying pan, add the sea bass and cook for 2–3 minutes on each side, depending on thickness.

To serve, add the potatoes to the broth and heat through, then season with salt, pepper and a squeeze of lemon juice to taste. Ladle the soup into bowls and place the sea bass fillets on top. Serve with the Aioli on the side.

Serves 6

CHILLED ROCKET AND YOGHURT SOUP WITH CRAB

I came across this light and refreshing soup while working in Sydney a few years back. It's perfect for a hot summer's day. Buy dressed crabs for this. You can use the white meat for the soup and spread the brown meat on toast with a squeeze of lemon to enjoy on the side.

Rocket is easily available in most supermarkets, sold in 'pillow packs' of 100g. Choose from either broad leaf or the narrow-leaf variety, commonly known as wild rocket. It's also a very simple salad leaf to grow at home, as it self-seeds easily and needs little more than regular watering to grow in abundance.

$1^1/_2$ tablespoons olive oil
1 leek, white part only, finely chopped
500g (1 pound 2 ounces) floury potatoes, peeled and diced
750ml (3 cups) light chicken stock
200g (7 ounces) rocket
300g ($1^1/_4$ cups) Greek yoghurt
2 small dressed crabs
1 cucumber, peeled, seeded and sliced into strips
Sea salt and freshly ground black pepper

Heat the olive oil in a saucepan, add the leek, potatoes and a pinch of sea salt, then cover and cook over a low heat for about 10 minutes, until the leek is soft. Pour in the stock and cook for 15–20 minutes, until the potatoes are tender. Set aside to cool.

Meanwhile, add the rocket to a large pan of boiling water, simmer for just 1 minute, then drain and refresh in iced water. Drain again and squeeze out the excess water. Chop up the rocket and add it to the soup; the soup needs to be cold in order to keep the vibrant green of the rocket.

Whiz the soup in a blender until smooth, then pour it into a bowl and stir in the yoghurt. If the soup is too thick, add a little more stock or water. Season with sea salt and black pepper and chill thoroughly.

Ladle the soup into bowls and top with the white crabmeat and cucumber strips. Serve with brown crabmeat toasts, if liked.

Serves 4

SALADS

GRILLED TUNA WITH SICILIAN POTATO SALAD

I inherited this recipe from my good friend and Eagle colleague, Tom Norrington-Davies, whose adaptation of this simple, saucy salad appears in *Real Pub Food* (Absolute Press, 2001). As Tom points out, it is vital to use good fresh tuna, not canned, and waxy new potatoes such as Charlotte. You could also successfully use other robust, meaty fish, such as swordfish or shark.

1kg (2¼ pounds) waxy potatoes, peeled and
   cut into chunks
400g (14 ounces) canned peeled plum
   tomatoes
8 tablespoons extra virgin olive oil
2 garlic cloves, thinly sliced
2 red onions, thinly sliced
Juice of 1 lemon
1 teaspoon sugar
½ teaspoon dried chilli flakes, or to taste
4 x 150g (5-ounce) tuna steaks, cut 1.5cm
   (⅔ inch) thick
A bunch of flat-leaf parsley, chopped
Sea salt and freshly ground black pepper

Cook the potatoes in boiling salted water until they are tender but still hold their shape. Drain and place in a bowl, then set aside.

Drain the canned tomatoes and squeeze out all the excess liquid.

Heat 3 tablespoons of the olive oil in a thick-bottomed pan. Add the garlic and fry until soft and translucent, then add the onions and cook just for a minute or two, until they have wilted. Add the drained tomatoes, lemon juice and sugar. Remove from the heat and pour this mixture over the potatoes. Mix with 3 tablespoons of the remaining olive oil. Season with sea salt and pepper and stir in the dried chilli. The salad can be as hot or as mild as you like.

To cook the tuna, heat a ridged grill pan over a high heat. Rub the tuna steaks with the remaining olive oil and season with salt and pepper. Place in the smoking-hot pan and sear for 1 minute on each side, then let them rest for another minute or so off the heat. The tuna will be medium rare, the best way to eat it.

Transfer the tuna to warm plates, scatter over the chopped parsley and drizzle with a little extra olive oil. Serve with the potato salad.

Serves 4

SALAD NICOISE

Strictly speaking, a salad niçoise is simply a salad that comes from Nice. Generally, however, there is a core of ingredients that are always present, including tuna, tomatoes, olives and eggs. The only thing common to all good niçoise salads is that the ingredients should be fresh and of the highest quality. This is the version I like to make.

The best canned tuna comes from Spain, so I use Spanish bonito or yellowfin tuna in olive oil. The tomatoes must be ripe plum tomatoes and the olives tiny black ones, ideally from Nice. The eggs should be soft boiled. I also think that the type of lettuce is important. Only Cos or Little Gem will do, as they are robust and will stay crisp under the weight of the other ingredients.

500g (1 pound 2 ounces) waxy new potatoes, scrubbed
150g (5 ounces) green beans, such as broad, French or runner beans
6 free-range eggs
1 tablespoon lemon juice
100ml (scant $^{1}/_{2}$ cup) extra virgin olive oil
6 tomatoes
2 tablespoons capers, drained
120g ($^{2}/_{3}$ cup) small black olives
1 Cos or 2 Little Gem lettuces, leaves torn
200g (7 ounces) canned tuna in olive oil
12 anchovy fillets
Sea salt and freshly ground black pepper

Boil the potatoes in salted water until they are tender. Drain and leave them to cool a little, then slice in half.

Cook the beans in boiling salted water until tender, then drain. Plunge them into cold water to cool them rapidly, so they keep their colour and crunch.

Bring another pan of water to the boil, add the eggs and cook for 6 minutes; this should give slightly runny yolks. Cool immediately under cold running water and peel as soon as possible; the shell will come off more easily that way. Cut the eggs lengthways in half.

Whisk together the lemon juice and olive oil in a bowl and season with sea salt and pepper. Add the slightly warm potatoes; they will absorb the dressing better while warm. Slice each tomato lengthways into quarters and add to the bowl. Mix in the green beans, capers, olives and lettuce, then introduce the tuna, drained of its oil. Toss around and divide between plates, or simply pile on to a platter. Top with the anchovy fillets and halved eggs.

Serves 6

WARM SALAD OF SMOKED EEL, BACON AND POTATO

I think smoked eel is the most sublime of smoked fish. Miles removed from the rubbery jellied eel of London fish stalls, it has a rich, subtle flavour that works so well with salty bacon. I'd serve this as a first course for a dinner party.

600g (1¼ *pounds*) *waxy new potatoes, scrubbed*
200g (7 *ounces*) *smoked eel fillet*
12 *smoked streaky bacon rashers*
A bunch of watercress, tough stalks removed

For the dressing
1 *teaspoon Dijon mustard*
20ml (4 *teaspoons*) *white wine vinegar*
60ml (4 *tablespoons*) *extra virgin olive oil*
Sea salt and freshly ground black pepper

Preheat the oven to 200°C/400°F/Gas Mark 6. Cook the potatoes in boiling salted water until just tender, then drain and keep warm. Slice the smoked eel fillet into 18 pieces.

To make the dressing, whisk together the mustard and vinegar, then add the olive oil in a slow stream. Season with sea salt and pepper.

Place the rashers of bacon on a baking tray, bake for 3–4 minutes, until crisp, then drain on kitchen paper. Lay the pieces of eel fillet on the tray and warm in the oven for 3 minutes.

Slice the warm potatoes into a bowl and add the watercress. Toss gently with the vinaigrette to coat, then divide the mixture between 6 plates. Place 3 pieces of eel on each plate and top with 2 rashers of bacon. Serve immediately.

Serves 6 as a first course

PICKLED HERRING WITH POTATOES, CUCUMBER AND CREAMY MUSTARD DRESSING

This is a light and creamy Scandinavian-style salad. I use Bismarck herrings for this, a raw herring pickled in spiced vinegar. Add the pickled onions from the tub along with the fish.

1 cucumber, thinly sliced
1 tablespoon caster sugar
1 teaspoon sea salt
500g (1 pound 2 ounces) waxy new potatoes,
*   scrubbed*
500g (1 pound 2 ounces) pickled herrings,
*   preferably Bismarck*
Freshly ground black pepper

For the dressing
200ml (scant 1 cup) double cream
2 tablespoons Pommery grain mustard
2 tablespoons lemon juice

First make the dressing. Combine the cream, mustard and lemon juice in a bowl and whisk until the mixture holds a soft peak. Leave in the fridge while you prepare the salad.

Toss the cucumber slices with the sugar and salt in a sieve placed over a bowl. Leave for half an hour to extract some of the liquid from the cucumber. Meanwhile, cook the potatoes in boiling salted water until tender, then drain and set aside to cool. Gently squeeze the excess liquid from the cucumber slices and dry them on a tea towel or kitchen paper.

Slice the herring fillets into 2cm ($^3/_4$ inch) strips. Halve the potatoes and mix them with the cucumber and the dressing. Season to taste with pepper; it may not need any more salt. Serve immediately, with Scandinavian crispbread.

Serves 4-6 as a starter

PRAWN, POTATO AND CUCUMBER SALAD

I have to thank my Uncle Keith for this recipe, as it's based on a salad he makes for Christmas lunch back home in Sydney. We always start the festivities with big platters of prawns, oysters and blue swimmer crabs, with Keith's secret-recipe lemon and cucumber relish. I have adapted this as a generous warm salad, extended with waxy new potatoes to absorb the sharp, lemony dressing. It's a perfect light summer lunch with crusty bread and a glass of crisp, dry white wine.

500g (1 pound 2 ounces) waxy new potatoes
1 cucumber
800g (1³/₄ pounds) cooked prawns, peeled

For the dressing
1 free-range egg yolk
1 tablespoon Dijon mustard
Grated zest of ¹/₂ lemon
50ml (3¹/₂ tablespoons) lemon juice
150ml (²/₃ cup) extra virgin olive oil
1 tablespoon chopped tarragon
Sea salt and freshly ground black pepper

Cook the potatoes in boiling salted water until tender, then drain and leave to cool. Peel off the skins. Peel the cucumber, cut it in half lengthways and remove the seeds. Cut the potatoes and cucumber into slices 5mm (¹/₄ inch) thick. Cut the prawns in half lengthways.

For the dressing, put the egg yolk, mustard, lemon zest and juice in a bowl and whisk together. While whisking continuously, slowly add the olive oil in a thin, steady stream until the mixture is emulsified. Stir in the tarragon and season to taste.

Toss the dressing with the potatoes, cucumber and prawns and serve.

Serves 6

PULPO A GALEGA

This is a little different from the dish found in bars and restaurants throughout Spain. Pulpo a galega is usually steamed discs of octopus, sprinkled with lemon juice and paprika and served on a wooden board – usually as a simple starter or on a bar alongside an array of tapas. I've always loved the flavours of this dish, sweet, sour and smoky, so I've turned it into a big salad, with tomatoes, potatoes and lots of fresh parsley. It makes a substantial lunch.

2 or 3 medium octopus, about 500g
   (1 pound 2 ounces) each
50ml (3^1/$_2$ tablespoons) extra virgin olive oil
2 garlic cloves, crushed
500g (1 pound 2 ounces) waxy new potatoes,
   scrubbed
6 ripe plum tomatoes, sliced lengthways
   into quarters
1 red onion, finely sliced
100g (^{2}/$_3$ cup) black olives
A small bunch of parsley, leaves picked but
   with a little of the stalk left intact

For the dressing
2 teaspoons smoked sweet paprika
4 tablespoons lemon juice
1 teaspoon sea salt
Freshly ground black pepper
200ml (scant ^{1}/$_2$ cup) extra virgin olive oil

To clean the octopus, use a sharp knife to cut the tentacles away from the head just under the shell-like beak, then put them in a bowl of salted water. Rub them vigorously; the salt will help dislodge any sand caught in the suckers. Turn the body inside out, remove and discard all the internal organs and wash under cold running water. Some cooks advocate skinning the octopus but I think the skin adds flavour and texture. Slice the body and tentacles into 1cm (^{1}/$_2$ inch) strips. (You could ask your fishmonger to do all this, if you prefer.)

Heat the olive oil in a pan, add the garlic and octopus and stir over a high heat for a minute to seal. Cover the pan, reduce the heat and cook gently for about 1^1/$_2$ hours, until the octopus is tender. It will sweat in its own liquid. Remove from the heat and leave to cool a little in the pan.

While the octopus is cooking, cook the potatoes in boiling salted water until tender, then drain and keep warm. Make the dressing by whisking together the paprika, lemon juice, salt and a grinding of pepper in a large bowl, then gradually whisking in the olive oil.

Cut the potatoes in half and add them to the dressing. Drain the octopus, reserving a couple of tablespoons of the cooking liquor, and add it to the bowl of potatoes with the reserved liquor. Mix in the tomatoes, onion and olives, then toss with the parsley. Serve with lots of crusty fresh bread.

Serves 4

RUSSIAN SALAD

This is a favourite salad all over Europe. The French, Italians and Russians have slightly differing versions. I add peeled brown shrimps to it, the type most commonly used in potted shrimps, though sweet peeled Atlantic prawns are an acceptable substitute. I love to eat this with a dressed crab and an extra dollop of mayonnaise.

It's important to cook all the vegetables separately and in strict order. Always do the green beans first, as they discolour if not cooked in fresh water, peas next, then carrots. Cook the potatoes separately.

200g (7 ounces) French beans, cut into 1cm
  (¹/₂ inch) lengths
200g (7 ounces) peas
200g (7 ounces) carrots, cut into 1cm
  (¹/₂ inch) dice
900g (2 pounds) waxy potatoes, peeled,
  cut into 1cm (¹/₂ inch) dice and rinsed
200g (7 ounces) peeled brown shrimps
3 free-range eggs, hard boiled and chopped
4 spring onions, finely sliced
100ml (scant ¹/₂ cup) Mayonnaise
  (see page 152)
100ml (scant ¹/₂ cup) soured cream or
  crème fraîche
Sea salt and freshly ground black pepper

Bring a large pan of salted water to the boil. Plunge the beans into the water and cook until just tender, then remove with a slotted spoon and refresh under cold running water. Next cook the peas until tender and refresh them under cold running water, too. Add the carrots to the pot and cook until *al dente*, then drain and set aside to cool. In another pan, simmer the potatoes in salted water until just cooked, then drain and set aside to cool.

Put all the vegetables into a large bowl and add the shrimps, eggs and spring onions. Stir in the mayonnaise and soured cream or crème fraîche and mix gently until all the vegetables are coated. Season with sea salt and pepper.

Serves 4

SEA TROUT, POTATO AND RADICCHIO SALAD WITH SAFFRON DRESSING

This salad makes a perfect spring lunch, with its pastel shades of pink, pale green and yellow. I use Jersey Royal potatoes, as they are the best partners for the first wild sea trout.

As this salad is made with raw trout, it's vital that you purchase the freshest one you can get your hands on. If you are at all squeamish about eating raw fish, though, you can poach it lightly in advance.

600g (1¼ pounds) waxy new potatoes, scrubbed
1 avocado, peeled, stoned and cut into 2cm (³/₄ inch) dice
2 small heads of radicchio, leaves separated
700g (1½ pounds) sea trout fillets, pinbones removed

For the saffron dressing
A pinch of saffron strands
1 free-range egg yolk
1 tablespoon Dijon mustard
2 tablespoons white wine vinegar
300ml (1¼ cups) extra virgin olive oil
Sea salt and freshly ground black pepper

Cook the potatoes in boiling salted water until tender, then drain and leave to cool. Meanwhile, make the dressing. Soak the saffron threads in 2 tablespoons of warm water for 20 minutes. Combine the mixture with the egg yolk, mustard and vinegar in a bowl and whisk until smooth. Whisking continuously, add the oil in a steady stream until the mixture is thick and emulsified. Season to taste with sea salt and pepper. Slice the potatoes into 2cm (³/₄ inch) discs and combine them with the avocado and radicchio leaves in a bowl. Using a sharp knife, cut the trout fillets into thin, wide slices on the diagonal, lifting the slices off the skin and adding them to the bowl as you go. Drizzle over some of the dressing and gently toss the salad. Divide between serving plates and serve the extra dressing on the side.

Serves 8 as a starter, 4 as a main course

CEVICHE WITH AVOCADO SALSA AND SWEET POTATO MASH

Originally from Peru, ceviche can be found all over Latin America. In ancient times, Peruvians ate raw fish when firewood was hard to come by and they seasoned it with bitter limes and hot pepper. The fish is 'cooked' by the acidity of the lime juice. It is usually served with mashed sweet potato and sweetcorn or an avocado salsa.

Many fish are suitable for ceviche. I mostly use a firm white fish, such as halibut or sea bass, but tuna, salmon and scallops are superb.

250g (9 ounces) very fresh, firm-fleshed fish fillets, skinned
1 bay leaf
Juice of 3 limes
Sea salt and freshly ground black pepper
Sweet Potato Mash (see page 150), to serve

For the avocado salsa
2 garlic cloves, finely sliced
1 large, ripe avocado, peeled, stoned and diced
2 tablespoons extra virgin olive oil
250g (9 ounces) ripe tomatoes, seeded and chopped
1 red onion, finely chopped
A bunch of coriander, roughly chopped
2 red chillies, seeded and chopped

Cut the fish into strips about 2cm ($^3/_4$ inch) long and 1cm ($^1/_2$ inch) thick. Put the strips into a bowl, season lightly with salt and pepper, then tuck in the bay leaf and pour over the lime juice. Cover and leave in the fridge to marinate for 2 hours, turning the fish once or twice.

Once the fish is opaque, drain it well and set aside.

Make the salsa just before serving. Simply combine all the ingredients in a bowl and mix well, then season with salt and pepper

Arrange the salsa on serving plates and top with the fish. Serve immediately, with the sweet potato mash on the side.

Serves 4

SOUSED HERRING WITH POTATO SALAD

Herrings are caught in vast numbers in the cold waters of the Atlantic and North Sea, and northern Europeans have numerous ways of preparing them. I've eaten them grilled, fried, baked, stuffed, and also had the most delicious herring burger on the south coast of Sweden.

This recipe is a pickle in the Baltic tradition. Sweet and sour, like a rollmop, it is perfect with the creamy potato salad.

500g (1 pound 2 ounces) herring fillets
30g ($1^1/_2$ tablespoons) sea salt
30g (2 tablespoons) caster sugar

For the pickle
2 carrots, finely sliced
1 onion, finely sliced
2 garlic cloves, finely sliced
1 fennel bulb, finely sliced
300ml ($1^1/_4$ cups) good-quality white wine
* vinegar*
1.2 litres (5 cups) water
50g (3 tablespoons) sea salt
300g ($1^1/_2$ cups) aster sugar
1 teaspoon fennel seeds
10 black peppercorns

For the potato salad
500g (1 pound 2 ounces) waxy new potatoes
2 tablespoons soured cream
2 teaspoons grain mustard
1 tablespoon red wine vinegar
3 spring onions, finely sliced
Sea salt and freshly ground black pepper

Put the herring fillets in a wide dish, mix together the sea salt and sugar and spread them over the fish. Cover and refrigerate overnight.

The next day, wash the salt mixture from the fish fillets and pat them dry. Arrange them in a dish again, side by side.

Put all the pickling ingredients in a pan and bring to the boil. Pour the boiling liquid over the fillets, then leave to cool. Cover and refrigerate for 48 hours before use. (The fish will keep in the fridge, covered with liquid, for a week.)

For the potato salad, bring the potatoes to the boil in a large pan of salted water, then reduce the heat and simmer until tender. Drain and leave until cool enough to handle. Meanwhile, mix together all the remaining ingredients. Peel the potatoes and cut them into quarters. Fold the warm potatoes into the dressing and serve at room temperature, alongside the herring.

Serves 4

TARAMASALATA

A light and tasty Greek appetiser, real taramasalata is slightly smoky from the cod's roe and pale pink in colour, not the scary, lurid shade you often find in tubs in the supermarket. Quick and easy to make in a food processor, it is an essential part of a mezze table.

250g (9 ounces) floury potatoes
250g (9 ounces) smoked cod's roe
1 onion, chopped
2 thick slices of day-old white bread
200ml (scant 1 cup) milk
400ml (1³/₄ cups) olive oil
Juice of 2 lemons, or to taste
Sea salt and freshly ground black pepper

Boil the potatoes in their skins in plenty of salted water until they are tender. Drain and leave until cool enough to handle, then peel them. Skin the cod's roe and put it in a food processor with the onion. Purée until you have a smooth paste. Cut the crusts off the bread and soak the slices in the milk, then squeeze out the liquid. Add the bread to the food processor and continue to purée.

Gradually pour in the olive oil in a slow, steady stream – not too fast or the mixture may split. Add the lemon juice, a little at a time, until you have it as lemony as you like, and season with sea salt and pepper.
Serve with hot pita bread.

Serves 6-8

POACHED

LOBSTER AND CHIPS

Here is the dish that inspired the whole book. I've always thought this was the perfect marriage, as I love the idea of the most exclusive of shellfish partnered with the humble spud. It got me thinking about the numerous combinations of fish and potatoes and just how wonderfully they can be brought together.

To my mind, the best way to eat lobster is to keep it as simple as possible. I have a purist outlook and don't like it to be mucked about, so no creamy sauces or overpowering dressings, please. Simply poached with mayonnaise or grilled with herb butter (see page 96), lobster is unbeatable with chips and a green salad.

The ideal cooking liquid for lobsters is seawater; second best is heavily salted tap water – 40g (2 tablespoons) of salt to 1 litre (4 cups) of water. Make sure you have your largest pot and never use less than 5 litres (5 quarts) of water. The lobsters need to be completely immersed and the water temperature maintained.

5 litres (5 quarts) water
200g ($^3/_4$ cup) sea salt
2 lobsters, weighing about 800g
  ($1^3/_4$ pounds) each

To serve
Chips (see page 147)
Mayonnaise (see page 152)

Put the water and salt in a large pot and bring to a rolling boil. Plunge the lobsters head first into the water and cover the pot to bring it back to the boil quickly. Simmer the lobsters uncovered for 8 minutes per 500g (1 pound 2 ounces) plus 5 minutes (so 800g/$1^3/_4$ pound lobsters will take about 12 minutes). Start timing from when the water returns to the boil.

When the lobsters are done, lift them from the water and leave until cool enough to handle. Place on a chopping board and cut through the middle of the head with a large, heavy knife, bringing it down between the eyes. Turn the lobster around and then cut right through the middle of the tail to split it in half. Crack open the claws with the back of the knife, using the heavy end near the handle. Remove the intestinal thread running through the back of the lobster and the bony sac inside the head.

Put a lobster half on each plate and serve with chips and mayonnaise on the side.

Serves 4

SKATE AND POTATO TERRINE

I used to make this terrine regularly when working at the Brackenbury restaurant in west London, run by Adam and Katie Robinson. I love the sweetness of skate; it works so well with the crunch and piquancy of gherkins and capers and is as fine and tasty cold as it is hot.

Some people think terrines are tricky or laborious to make but this is so quick and simple. The gelatinous nature of the skate helps to hold all the ingredients firmly together, though it needs to be cut without applying too much pressure. I use a very sharp knife and cut with a sawing motion.

This terrine makes a great summer lunch with crusty bread and a big salad.

1 litre (4 cups) water
200ml (scant 1 cup) white wine
Juice of $\frac{1}{2}$ lemon
2 tablespoons chopped parsley, stalks
 reserved
1kg (2$\frac{1}{4}$ pounds) skate wings on the bone
500g (1 pound 2 ounces) large waxy
 potatoes, boiled and peeled
8-10 baby gherkins
2 teaspoons capers, drained
2 shallots
1 tablespoon Dijon mustard
A little olive oil
Sea salt and freshly ground black pepper

Put the water, white wine, lemon juice and parsley stalks in a large, wide pan and bring to the boil. Season with salt and pepper and add the skate wings. Poach over a low heat for 12–15 minutes, until the flesh comes away from the bone easily. Drain and set aside to cool just a little, then pull the fish in strips off the central bone. It will be pretty untidy but that doesn't really matter.

Thinly slice the cooked potatoes, put them in a bowl and gently mix in the fish. Chop together the gherkins, capers and shallots and put them in a small bowl. Mix in the mustard and chopped parsley and lubricate with enough olive oil to make a paste.

Line a 900g (2-pound) terrine mould or loaf tin, or a bowl, with cling film, making sure there is enough left hanging over the sides to fold over the top of the terrine. Place a layer of fish and potato slices in the terrine and top with some of the parsley mixture; alternate these layers until the terrine is full. Fold the cling film over the terrine and place a weight on top – ideally another terrine or a plate with a couple of cans on top. Leave in the fridge overnight.

To serve, unmould the terrine and cut into slices with a very sharp knife.

**Serves about 10 as a starter,
6 for lunch**

SALT COD BRANDADE

Brandade de morue is a speciality of Provence and is traditionally eaten around feast days – particularly Christmas Eve, when it serves as a humble evening meal before people embark on the celebrations next day.

This light and fluffy white purée is often served with croûtons or in warm puff pastry cases but I usually accompany it with crusty bread, a sharp green salad and a bowl of small black olives on the side. The olive oil is integral to the flavour of this dish, so it should be of the highest quality.

2 large waxy potatoes, weighing 400g (14 ounces) in total, peeled and cut into chunks
700g (1$\frac{1}{2}$ pounds) salt cod, soaked for 12 hours or overnight in several changes of water
3 garlic cloves, crushed
225ml (1 scant cup) warm milk
225ml (1 scant cup) warm extra virgin olive oil, plus a little extra for drizzling
Juice of 1 lemon
Sea salt and freshly ground black pepper

Place the potatoes in a pan of water with a small pinch of sea salt and bring to the boil. Reduce the heat to a simmer and cook until tender. Drain well, then mash and keep warm.

Meanwhile, drain the salt cod, put it in a large pan of fresh, unsalted water and place over a high heat. Just as the water begins to boil, remove the pan from the heat and leave for 5 minutes to poach the cod gently. Remove the fish from the pan with a slotted spoon and leave to drain on a plate. When it is cool enough to handle, peel off the skin and remove any bones. Flake the fish into the mashed potato and add the garlic.

Alternately add the warm milk and olive oil to the mash, a little at a time, beating both in well until you have a light but slightly rough-textured purée. Add the lemon juice to taste, plus plenty of black pepper and maybe a little sea salt if necessary.

Pile into warmed bowls, drizzle with a little extra olive oil and serve.

Serves 6

SMOKED HADDOCK STOVIES WITH FRIED EGGS AND MUSTARD SAUCE

This is a fishy version of the Scots dish, stoved tatties. In Scotland potatoes are sometimes cooked very slowly in a pan on top of the stove with a little water and butter, so a crust forms on the bottom. You see these potato cakes regularly as bar meals in local pubs, often made with salt beef added to the potatoes.

The recipe here is a bit of a cheat. I pre-cook the ingredients, which makes the dish much quicker, and, of course, I am using fish not beef, but have a go – it works really well. Serve with a fried egg.

700g (1^1/$_2$ pounds) floury potatoes, peeled
   and cut into 2cm (^{3}/$_4$ inch) chunks
1 onion, sliced
400g (14 ounces) smoked haddock fillets
50g (3^1/$_2$ tablespoons) unsalted butter, plus
   extra for frying the eggs
4 free-range eggs
Sea salt and freshly ground black pepper

For the mustard sauce
300ml (1^1/$_4$ cups) double cream
2 tablespoons Dijon mustard

Put the potatoes and onion in a large pan of salted water and bring to the boil. Lower the heat to a simmer and gently place the haddock fillets on top of the potatoes. Poach the fish for 3 minutes or until opaque, then remove with a slotted spoon and set aside. Continue to cook the onion and potatoes until the potatoes are just done, then drain well and tip them into a bowl.

Preheat the oven to 200°C/Gas Mark 6.

Remove the skin and any bones from the fish, flake it into the potato and onion, then mix everything together with half the butter; you should aim for a chunky texture rather than a smooth mash. Season to taste.

Melt the remaining butter in a large ovenproof frying pan, then pour in the fishy mixture and shake the pan around to prevent it sticking. Cook over a medium heat, until golden underneath, then transfer to the oven. Bake for 10–15 minutes, until brown and crisp on top.

Meanwhile, for the sauce, put the cream and mustard in a pan, bring to the boil and simmer for 2–3 minutes. Season with salt and pepper to taste and keep warm.

Fry the eggs in a little extra butter. Turn the stovie out of the pan and divide it between 4 plates. Top each portion with an egg and spoon around the mustard sauce.

Serves 4

SMOKED HADDOCK WITH SAFFRON MASH AND POACHED EGG

This is a great brunch dish that has all the elements of comfort food: creamy mash topped with luscious flaky fish and a runny-yolked egg. Proper smoked haddock and mash has white fish and yellow mash, not the other way round.

4 x 200g (7-ounce) pieces of smoked haddock fillet
4 free-range eggs

For the mash
900g (2 pounds) floury potatoes, peeled and cut into chunks
200ml (scant 1 cup) milk
A generous pinch of saffron threads
100g (7 tablespoons) unsalted butter
Sea salt and freshly ground black pepper

For the court-bouillon
1.2 litres (5 cups) water
1 tablespoon white wine vinegar
1 bay leaf
A sprig of thyme
6 black peppercorns
A pinch of sea salt

Bring the potatoes to the boil in plenty of salted water. Reduce the heat to a simmer and cook until tender. Drain well, return to the pan and dry out over a low heat until all the water has evaporated. Warm the milk with the saffron, leave for a minute to infuse, then pour it over the potatoes while crushing them with a potato masher. Beat in the butter, season with salt and pepper, then cover and keep warm.

For the court-bouillon, put all the ingredients in a wide, shallow pan large enough to hold the fish and bring to the boil. Turn down to a simmer and lower in the fish. Poach very gently, uncovered, for about 5 minutes, until it is firm to the touch. Drain and keep warm.

You can poach the eggs in the court-bouillon, too. To do this, break an egg into a cup, bring the court-bouillon back to a simmer and stir it with a spoon to create a kind of whirlpool. Then gently drop in the egg. Once it has set a little, you can repeat with another egg. Poach them for about 3 minutes (they should only be soft poached, as the runny yolk serves as a dressing).

Divide the mash and the fish between 4 warm plates and top each portion with a poached egg.

Serves 4

MUSSEL, POTATO AND CAPER RAVIOLI

Ravioli needn't be a daunting prospect. I often cheat by using egg won ton or rice paper wrappers. Easily found in Asian grocer's shops, they can be kept in the freezer and used as and when you need them. They have the added advantage of being sturdier than pasta dough, so are less likely to split when you are filling and cooking them.

1kg (2¼ pounds) mussels
50ml (3½ tablespoons) olive oil
3 garlic cloves, finely chopped
300g (11 ounces) waxy potatoes, peeled and
    cut into 2cm (¾ inch) dice
1 tablespoon capers, drained and roughly
    chopped
50g (½ cup) pine nuts, lightly toasted in a
    dry frying pan
2 tablespoons chopped parsley
A packet of won ton wrappers
100g (7 tablespoons) unsalted butter
2 tablespoons chopped dill
Juice of ¼ lemon
Salt and freshly ground black pepper

Scrub the mussels to remove any sand or barnacles and pull out their beards – the hairy bit poking out of the shell. Tap any open mussels on the work surface to see if they close; if they don't, be sure to discard them.

Bring 50ml (3½ tablespoons) water to the boil in a large, heavy-based pan and add the mussels. Slam down the lid and let the mussels steam for about 5 minutes, until they are all open. Transfer the mussels to a colander placed over a bowl and leave until cool enough to handle, then pick them from their shells and chop roughly. Strain the cooking liquid through a fine sieve and set aside.

Heat the olive oil in a frying pan, add the garlic and cook over a low heat until soft, being careful not to let it brown. Add the potatoes and about 4 tablespoons of the mussel liquid, then cover and cook over a low heat for 10–15 minutes, until the potatoes are tender. Increase the heat to medium, uncover the pan and cook until most of the liquid has evaporated. Stir in the mussels, capers and pine nuts and season with salt and pepper. Leave to cool, then stir in the parsley.

Lay a won ton wrapper on a work surface. Put a generous teaspoon of the filling mixture in the middle, brush the edges lightly with water and then put another wrapper on top. Press the edges together to seal. Repeat with the remaining filling and wrappers. Keep the ravioli under a tea towel until they are all done.

Bring a large pan of salted water to the boil. Meanwhile, in a separate pan, melt the butter, then stir in the dill and lemon juice. Season with salt and pepper

Drop the ravioli into the boiling water and simmer very gently for 5 minutes or until tender. Drain well, toss them gently in the dill butter and serve immediately

Serves 6

TUNA CONFIT

A speciality of southwest France, confit simply means to cook in fat. It is one of the oldest methods of preserving food. Most often the term is applied to duck, goose or pork, slowly cooked in its own fat, then stored, still in its fat, in Kilner jars or an earthenware pot. Tuna fares very well under this treatment, though a light olive oil (the fat) is the traditional cooking medium for it. Serve your confit warm (it's not that nice hot) with a simple salad, or leave it to cool and toss it into a salad niçoise (see page 36).

500ml (2 cups) olive oil
10 black peppercorns
1 teaspoon sea salt
1 red chilli
2 bay leaves
Pared zest of 1 lemon
1kg (2¹/₄ pounds) tuna belly

Put the olive oil, peppercorns, salt, chilli, bay leaves and lemon zest in a pan wide enough to hold the tuna and bring to simmering point. Then immerse the fish in the oil. It should be completely covered. Cook over the lowest possible heat for 30 minutes; the surface should only barely ripple. Remove from the heat and leave the tuna to cool in the oil.

You can use it straight away or it will keep in the fridge, covered, for a week.

Serves 6

MUSSELS, CHIPS AND MAYONNAISE

Strictly speaking, this recipe shouldn't be in this chapter, as it isn't poached, but it's such a classic I had to squeeze it in somewhere. Wherever you go in Belgium you will find moules frites on the menu.

A portion usually consists of around a kilo (a couple of pounds) of mussels that have been cooked in white wine with celery or tomatoes and herbs, served with thin pommes frites and mayonnaise and washed down with the local beer. *Moules à volonté* on the menu is all you can eat; the waiters keep bringing them out until you tell them to stop.

2kg (4^1/$_2$ pounds) mussels
50g (3^1/$_2$ tablespoons) unsalted butter
1 onion, sliced
1 celery stalk, sliced
200ml (scant 1 cup) white wine
100ml (scant ^{1}/$_2$ cup) double cream
2 tablespoons chopped parsley

To serve
Chips (see page 147)
Mayonnaise (see page 152)

Scrub the mussels to remove any sand or barnacles off and pull out the hairy beards with a sharp tug. Discard any open mussels that don't close when tapped on the work surface.

In a very large pan, melt the butter over a medium heat, then add the onion and celery and sauté until soft. Tip in the mussels and white wine and quickly jam on the lid. Turn the heat up high and cook for 4–5 minutes, turning the mussels occasionally, until all the shells are open.

Transfer the mussels to a warm bowl with tongs or a slotted spoon. Pour the cream into the mussel liquor and heat until bubbling. Throw in the parsley, swirl around and pour the mixture over the mussels. Serve at once, with chips and mayonnaise.

Serves 4

POACHED SEA TROUT, NEW POTATOES AND SAMPHIRE

This is a perfect dish for a lazy summer lunch. Samphire, which is also known as sea asparagus, grows on the salt marshes of the Essex and Norfolk coast and is available from fishmongers in the summer months. It is very salty, so you need to blanch it in unsalted water.

I use a fish kettle for this dish but if you don't have one, a large, deep roasting tin lined with a double layer of aluminium foil, which is strong enough to lift the fish, will do nicely. The trout can be poached and the salad made beforehand, so there is no last-minute rushing around. You can relax and enjoy your day.

1 sea trout, weighing about 1.5kg
   ($3^1/_4$ pounds)
750g (1 pound 10 ounces) Jersey Royal
   potatoes, scrubbed
300g (11 ounces) samphire
$^1/_2$ quantity of Mayonnaise (see page 152)

For the court-bouillon
3.5 litres ($3^1/_2$ quarts) water
150ml ($^2/_3$ cup) white wine vinegar
1 carrot, sliced
1 onion, sliced
1 bay leaf
A few parsley stalks
10 black peppercorns
1 teaspoon salt

Put all the court-bouillon ingredients in a fish kettle, bring to the boil and simmer for 10 minutes. Carefully drop the sea trout into it, bring back to the boil, then reduce the heat and simmer, covered, for 10 minutes (if you prefer the fish medium rare, reduce the cooking time to 5 minutes). Take the fish kettle off the heat and leave the fish to rest for 10 minutes.

Cook the potatoes in boiling salted water until tender, then drain and set aside.

Bring a large pan of unsalted water to the boil and plunge the samphire into it. Cook for 1 minute, then drain the samphire and refresh under cold running water. Drain again. When the potatoes are cool enough to handle, slice them in half and put them in a bowl with the samphire. Toss with the mayonnaise.

Take the trout out of the court-bouillon and drain well. Serve on a large platter, with the potatoes and samphire.

Serves 6

FRIED

VIETNAMESE PRAWN CAKES

I first encountered these tasty street snacks in the south of Vietnam, mostly in villages on the Mekong Delta. Like most Vietnamese spring rolls and pancakes, they are served with nuoc cham, a sweet and spicy fish sauce, and wrapped in crisp lettuce leaves. They are equally good hot or cold, so could be served as a starter or taken off on a picnic.

Use as much or as little chilli as you like in the nuoc cham. It's meant to be a spiky as opposed to a hot sauce.

500g (1 pound 2 ounces) large raw prawns
300g (11 ounces) plain flour
200ml (scant 1 cup) water
1 teaspoon sea salt
1 medium potato, peeled and sliced into
   shoestrings
200ml (scant 1 cup) vegetable oil
Freshly ground black pepper
Lettuce leaves, to serve

For the nuoc cham
4 tablespoons lime juice
3 tablespoons Thai fish sauce
2 tablespoons water
1 teaspoon palm sugar or brown sugar
1/2–1 red chilli, seeded and finely sliced

To make the nuoc cham, combine all the ingredients in a bowl and stir until the sugar has dissolved. Set aside.

Pull the heads off the prawns, then peel off the shells. Use the tip of a sharp knife to remove the black intestinal vein from the back of each prawn. Wash the prawns and dry them well. Mash half of them coarsely in a pestle and mortar or a food processor and slice the remaining ones in half. Set aside.

Put the flour in a bowl and gradually add the water, stirring until you have a smooth batter the consistency of thick cream. Mix in the mashed prawns and season with the sea salt and some pepper. Stir well to combine, then add the potato.

In a deep saucepan, heat the vegetable oil to 180°C/350°F. With a shallow ladle, scoop up about a tablespoon of the batter, then press half a prawn into it and carefully lower it into the hot oil. Fry the cake for 1 minute, then turn it over and cook for a further minute, until the batter is lightly golden and the prawn turns pink. Repeat with the remaining mixture. Drain on kitchen paper and serve each prawn cake wrapped up in a lettuce leaf, accompanied by the nuoc cham.

Makes 20-24

TEMPURA PRAWNS WITH SOY DIPPING SAUCE

It is best to make this Japanese speciality with hungry friends just waiting to eat it and demolishing each batch as it leaves the pan.

The batter should be made immediately before use and preferably mixed with chopsticks, so it's okay if it's a little lumpy. It gives a light, lacy coating. Only cook small batches at a time so as not to lower the temperature of the oil, or the prawns will stew rather than fry. Let the oil heat up again before adding the next batch of prawns.

Serve this with Straw Potatoes (see page 90).

30 large raw prawns
Sunflower oil for deep-frying
1 free-range egg
250ml (1 cup) iced water
150g (1 cup) plain flour, sifted
$^1/_2$ teaspoon bicarbonate of soda

For the soy dipping sauce
1 tablespoon sugar
2 tablespoons rice vinegar
2 tablespoons light soy sauce
2 teaspoons grated fresh ginger

First make the soy dipping sauce. Put the sugar, vinegar and soy sauce in a small bowl and stir until the sugar has dissolved. Add the grated ginger and set aside. This sauce will keep well in an airtight jar in the fridge for a few days.

Clean the prawns by pulling off the heads and peeling off the shells, leaving the tail intact. With the tip of a small sharp knife, cut down the back of each prawn, though not all the way through, and remove the black intestinal vein. Flatten the prawns with the heel of your hand to 'butterfly' them.

Heat some oil to 180°C/350°F in a deep-fat fryer or a deep saucepan. Meanwhile, make the batter. Whisk the egg lightly and pour in the ice-cold water. Add the flour and bicarbonate of soda in one go and stir until loosely combined.

Dip the prawns in the batter one at a time, lower them carefully into the oil and fry in batches for about 3 minutes, until crisp and golden. Drain well on lots of kitchen paper and serve with the dipping sauce.

Serves 4

DEEP-FRIED SALT COD CAKES

These delicious little Portuguese salt cod puffs, *pasteis de bacalhau*, make a great snack with an aperitif. I've eaten a ton of these in Lisbon and the Portuguese cafés of south London, hot and salty with a big dollop of garlicky mayonnaise, all washed down with a cold Sagres lager.

I mostly use cod that I've salted myself for these cakes (see page 10). As it's usually only under a blanket of salt for a couple of days, it doesn't dry out too much, desalinates quickly, and retains some of its sweetness.

This recipe makes a fairly large batch but if you can't get through all of them in one sitting, they are just as good cold.

350g (12 ounces) salt cod, soaked for 12 hours or overnight in several changes of water (or use home-made salt cod, see page 10)
700g (1^1/$_2$ pounds) waxy potatoes, peeled and cut into 3–4cm (1^1/$_4$–1^1/$_2$ inch) chunks
3 garlic cloves, peeled but left whole
2 free-range eggs
2 tablespoons chopped parsley
1 teaspoon plain flour
750ml (3 cups) sunflower or vegetable oil for deep-frying
Sea salt and freshly ground black pepper

Drain the salt cod and put it in a large pan of fresh water. Bring to the boil and simmer for 20 minutes, until the flesh is pulling away from the bone. Remove with a slotted spoon and set aside to cool a little.

Carefully put the potatoes and garlic into the same water and simmer until the potatoes are tender. Don't boil, or the potatoes will disintegrate and the resulting mixture will be gluey. Meanwhile, peel off the skin and pick out the bones from the salt cod, then shred the flesh.

Drain the potatoes very thoroughly; they need to be dry so that the cakes fry well. Mash the potatoes and garlic cloves in a bowl with a potato masher, then mix in the fish, eggs, parsley and flour. If the mixture seems too wet, add a little extra flour. Season to taste. Shape the cod cakes into little ovals with the aid of 2 tablespoons and set aside.

Heat the oil in a deep-fat fryer or a deep saucepan to 180°C/350°F. The best way to tell if it's hot enough is to add a small amount of the mixture; it should slowly go golden brown. Cook the cakes in batches that easily fit into the pan. Don't overcrowd it, as this reduces the heat and the cakes won't crisp. Fry for 3–4 minutes until golden, turning if necessary. Drain on kitchen paper and serve with Aioli (see page 152).

Makes about 24

DEEP-FRIED WHITEBAIT

Whitebait is the name for a young herring or sprat. They are at their best when deep-fried to a delectable crisp morsel and enlivened with a few drops of lemon juice. As they are eaten whole, heads, insides and all, it's best to get the smallest fish you can, no more than 5cm (2 inches) long. The bigger they are, the less pleasant to eat.

Fresh whitebait can be bought from fishmongers in the summer months, and you can also buy it frozen. Be sure to thaw it slowly in the fridge on kitchen paper. I serve deep-fried whitebait with wedges of lemon, a bowl of Aioli (see page 152) and Straw Potatoes (see page 90) on the side.

1kg (2¼ pounds) fresh whitebait
Sunflower oil for deep-frying
150g (1 cup) plain flour
Sea salt and freshly ground black pepper

To serve
2 lemons, cut into wedges
Aioli

Wash the whitebait well in cold water, then drain and pat dry with kitchen paper. Heat the oil to 180°C/350°F in a deep-fat fryer or a deep saucepan. Put the flour in a large bowl, season with salt and pepper and mix to combine. Add the whitebait and toss to coat them well, then remove and shake of any excess flour.

Fry the fish in batches until crisp and brown; they will curl and float to the top. Remove them with a slotted spoon and transfer to a plate lined with kitchen paper. Keep warm in a low oven while frying the remaining whitebait. Serve immediately, with lemon wedges, the straw potatoes and a dollop of aioli.

Serves 4 generously

SAMOSAS

Samosas are usually a vegetarian snack but here I'm adding fish to the mix. I generally use a cheap white fish, such as ling or pollock, but you could really push the boat out and add white crabmeat if you were feeling flush.

500g (1 pound 2 ounces) floury potatoes
2 tablespoons vegetable oil
1 teaspoon mustard seeds
1 onion, finely chopped
1 tablespoon grated fresh ginger
1–2 green chillies, seeded and finely chopped
1 teaspoon ground coriander
1/2 teaspoon turmeric
1 teaspoon garam masala
1 teaspoon sea salt
250g (9 ounces) white fish fillets, skinned and cut into 2cm (3/4 inch) dice (or white crabmeat)
1–2 tablespoons lemon juice
4 tablespoons chopped coriander
Vegetable oil for deep-frying

For the pastry
300g (2 cups) plain flour
1/2 teaspoon sea salt
4 tablespoons vegetable oil
8 tablespoons water

First make the pastry. Sift the flour into a bowl, add the salt, then rub in the oil. When it starts to resemble breadcrumbs, gradually mix in the water to make a firm dough. Turn out on to a lightly floured surface and knead for about 5 minutes, until smooth. Cover and leave to rest for an hour in a cool place.

Boil the potatoes in their skins in plenty of salted water until just tender, then drain. When they are cool enough to handle, peel and cut into 1cm (1/2 inch) cubes.

Heat the oil in a pan, add the mustard seeds and fry until they pop. Add the onion, ginger and chilli and cook over a low heat for 5 minutes, until soft. Add the ground spices and sea salt, followed by the potatoes, and cook for 3 minutes. Remove from the heat, mix in the fish, lemon juice and coriander and leave to cool.

Divide the pastry into 8 balls. On a lightly floured surface, roll out each ball into a circle about 24cm (10 inches) in diameter. Cut the circle in half and brush the edges with water. Place a tablespoon of the mixture in the centre and fold the pastry to form a cone. Press down the edges to seal.

Heat some oil to 190°C/375°F in a deep-fat fryer or a deep saucepan. Cook the samosas in batches of 4 (it's important not to crowd the pan or lower the temperature too much). They should take about 7 or 8 minutes to puff up and become golden brown. Drain on kitchen paper and serve immediately.

Makes 16

SARDINE ESCABECHE WITH POTATO SALAD

This traditional Spanish pickling method can be applied to any oily fish, such as mackerel, herring and sardines. These are fish that move about in large shoals, so fishermen would often come back to port with more fresh fish than they could sell. This dish was a means of preserving them in the days before refrigeration. It's still a good way for home cooks to conserve any extra fish they may have. The fish will keep, covered, in the fridge for about a week. They make a fantastic snack on top of grilled or toasted bread, or served alongside a simple potato salad, as below.

Plain flour for dusting
24 sardines, scaled and gutted
200ml (scant 1 cup) olive oil
Sea salt and freshly ground black pepper

For the marinade
300ml (1¹/₄ cups) red wine vinegar
100ml (scant ¹/₂ cup) water
1 red onion, very thinly sliced
1 fennel bulb, very thinly sliced
4 garlic cloves, finely sliced
1 teaspoon coriander seeds
1 teaspoon fennel seeds

For the potato salad
500g (1 pound 2 ounces) waxy new potatoes
1 shallot, finely sliced
20ml (4 teaspoons) sherry vinegar
50ml (3¹/₂ teaspoons) extra virgin olive oil

To make the marinade, put all the ingredients in a pan and bring to the boil. Simmer for 5 minutes to let the flavours mingle, then remove from the heat.

Season the flour with salt and pepper and dust the sardines in it, shaking off any excess flour. Heat half the oil in a large pan, add the sardines and fry them gently until they are golden brown on both sides. Spread them out side by side in a shallow dish. Pour over the marinade and the remaining olive oil and set aside to cool. Cover and refrigerate for at least 24 hours.

For the salad, bring the potatoes to the boil in a large pan of salted water, then reduce the heat and simmer until tender. Meanwhile, mix the shallot with a pinch of sea salt and the vinegar and leave to marinate.

Drain the potatoes and leave until cool enough to handle, then peel them and cut them into quarters. Add the warm potatoes to the shallots, pour over the olive oil and stir around to combine. Check the seasoning. Serve the salad at room temperature, alongside the sardines.

Serves 6

FRITTATA ALLA MARINARA

This recipe is adapted from one in Alan Davidson's book, *North Atlantic Seafood* (Penguin, 1979). The original recipe comes from *Il cuoco galante*, the first real cookbook of Naples, published in 1765. I've added potatoes for a more robust and portable omelette. Note that the weight given for the clams and mussels is in their shells.

400g (14 ounces) clams
500g (1 pound 2 ounces) mussels
500g (1 pound 2 ounces) waxy potatoes,
  peeled and cut into 1cm ($^1/_2$ inch) cubes
4 tablespoons olive oil
1 garlic clove, crushed
400g (14 ounces) raw prawns, shell on
6 free-range eggs
2 tablespoons chopped parsley
Sea salt and freshly ground black pepper

Wash the clams under cold running water to remove any grit or sand. Scrub the mussels to remove any sand or barnacles and pull out their beards – the hairy bit poking out of the shell. Tap any open mussels or clams on the work surface to see if they close; discard them if they don't. Set the shellfish aside.

Cook the potatoes in plenty of boiling salted water until tender, then drain and set aside. Heat half the olive oil in a large pan, add the garlic and cook gently until golden. Add the mussels and clams, cover the pan and raise the heat to medium. Cook for about 5 minutes, until the shellfish open. Remove them with a slotted spoon and leave until cool enough to handle, then pick the meat from the shells. Strain the liquor into a clean pan, bring to the boil and add the prawns. Cook for 2–3 minutes, until they change colour, then remove from the heat. Peel the prawns.

In a bowl, beat the eggs with the parsley. Strain the broth again and add 2 tablespoons of it to the eggs. Stir in the potatoes and shellfish, season with pepper but go easy on the salt; it will have plenty of salty flavour from the broth.

Heat the remaining olive oil in a large frying pan and pour in the mixture. Cook gently until set underneath and only slightly liquid on top. To turn the frittata, put a large plate on top of it, invert the omelette on to the plate, then slide it back into the pan to cook it underneath. If this seems a bit tricky, place it under a medium grill until set on top. To serve, turn the frittata out and cut it into wedges.

Serves 4-6

POPIAH

Popiah are a Malaysian street food in the Nonya style, a regional cuisine that borrows from Chinese and Indian traditions. They are pancakes spread with yellow bean paste and then wrapped round a spicy prawn and potato salad. The yellow bean paste is available in the UK from Chinese grocers.

2 tablespoons vegetable oil
1 teaspoon finely grated fresh ginger
2 garlic cloves, finely sliced
200g (7 ounces) peeled raw prawns, chopped
200g (7 ounces) waxy potatoes, peeled, grated and squeezed dry
1 carrot, grated
6 spring onions, finely sliced
200g (7 ounces) bean sprouts
1/2 small cucumber, grated
1–2 red chillies, seeded and finely sliced
Sea salt and freshly ground black pepper

For the pancakes
200g (1 1/3 cups) plain flour
1/2 teaspoon sea salt
2 free-range eggs, beaten
450ml (1 3/4 cups) water
2 tablespoons vegetable oil, plus extra for frying

For the soy and chilli dipping sauce
2 tablespoons sugar
2 tablespoons rice vinegar
2 tablespoons soy sauce
1 red chilli, seeded and thinly sliced

To serve
Yellow bean paste
12 crisp lettuce leaves
A small bunch of coriander
100g (1 cup) salted peanuts, chopped

First make the pancakes. Sift the flour and salt into a bowl, make a well in the centre and add the eggs. Whisk well, gradually adding the water and oil to make a thin batter. Leave to rest for 30 minutes.

Heat a 20cm (8-inch) non-stick frying pan and add a little oil. Tip away the excess, pour in a ladleful of the batter – just enough to make a thin pancake – and swirl it around to cover the base of the pan. Cook for 1–2 minutes, until lightly browned underneath, then turn it over to cook the other side. Repeat with the rest of the batter until you have 12 pancakes (you can stack them up while you cook the rest).

To make the sauce, mix the sugar, vinegar and soy sauce together until the sugar has dissolved, then stir in the chilli (the sauce will keep in an airtight jar in the fridge for a few days).

For the filling, heat the vegetable oil in a frying pan, add the ginger and garlic and fry for 1–2 minutes, until softened. Add the prawns and fry for a minute, then add the potatoes and carrot and fry for 2 minutes, until just tender. Remove from the heat and stir in the spring onions, bean sprouts, cucumber and chilli. Season with salt and pepper and leave to cool.

To assemble, spread each pancake with a smear of yellow bean paste, then top with a lettuce leaf and some of the filling. Add some coriander leaves and peanuts and roll up tightly. Serve with the dipping sauce.

Makes 12

SCALLOPS WITH BLACK PUDDING AND MASH

This is a simplified version of a dish created in the mid Nineties by the French chef, Bruno Loubet. He was looking for an affordable scallop dish for his Soho bistro and, by partnering scallops with the relatively inexpensive black pudding, he created an instant classic. It has been much copied, and deservedly so.

800g (1³/₄ pounds) floury potatoes, peeled
   and cut into chunks
150g (²/₃ cup) unsalted butter
150ml (²/₃ cup) warm milk
500g (1 pound 2 ounces) black pudding,
   cut into 12 slices
2 tablespoons vegetable oil
12 fresh scallops
Juice of ¼ lemon
1 tablespoon chopped parsley
1 garlic clove, finely chopped
Sea salt and freshly ground black pepper

Bring the potatoes to the boil in a pan of salted water, then lower the heat and simmer until tender. Drain well and return them to the pan over a low heat to let the excess water evaporate. Mash with the butter and warm milk, then season well with salt and pepper and keep warm.

Preheat the oven to 150°C/300°F/Gas Mark 2. Put the black pudding slices in a baking dish and heat through in the oven for about 15 minutes.

Heat the vegetable oil in a large frying pan, add the scallops and cook over a medium-high heat for about 2 minutes on each side, until firm and brown. Season with salt and pepper, squeeze over the lemon juice and mix in the parsley and garlic. Shake the pan to coat the scallops.

Divide the mashed potato between 4 plates and alternately arrange the scallops and the black pudding slices on top. Serve immediately with a crisp green salad.

Serves 4

WILD SALMON, JERSEY ROYALS AND WATERCRESS

This is one of my favourite dishes of early summer. The first of the wild salmon comes into the market at the beginning of June, just in time to catch the end of the Jersey Royal season. Any later and the potatoes will have grown to mid-size, when they don't seem to taste as sweet.

As wild salmon is rather expensive, you could substitute sea trout or organic salmon.

750g (1 pound 2 ounces) Jersey Royal
  potatoes, scraped clean
30g (2 tablespoons) unsalted butter
A splash of olive oil
4 x 200g (7-ounce) pieces of salmon fillet
Sea salt and freshly ground black pepper

For the watercress
Juice of ¼ lemon
25ml (2 tablespoons) extra virgin olive oil
150g (5 ounces) watercress, tough stalks
  removed

Cook the potatoes in boiling salted water until tender, then drain and keep warm.

Melt the butter in a large frying pan and add the olive oil. Season the fish with salt and pepper and, when the butter starts to bubble, add it to the pan, skin-side down. Fry for 3 minutes over a medium heat. The skin should be crisp by now, so turn the fillets over and cook for a further 2 minutes. The salmon should be slightly underdone.

Make a dressing by whisking together the lemon juice and olive oil with some salt and pepper to taste, then toss with the watercress.

Arrange the salmon and the potatoes on 4 warmed plates and serve immediately, with the watercress salad on the side.

Serves 4

MUM'S TUNA FISHCAKES

These fishcakes were a regular Friday-night tea for our family, occasionally making way for salmon and potato cakes if there was a can of salmon in the cupboard. They are ideal everyday family food – cheap, quick, easy and really tasty, yet not at all junky. We children couldn't get enough of them, and we always ate them with tomato ketchup and an added dash of Worcestershire sauce.

I use good canned Spanish tuna when I make these at home, but at the very least use tuna in olive oil; brined tuna has a nasty cat-foodiness about it.

500g (1 pound 2 ounces) floury potatoes, peeled and cut into chunks
400g (14 ounces) canned tuna in olive oil, drained
4 spring onions, finely sliced
2 tablespoons chopped parsley
A squeeze of lemon juice
Plain flour for dusting
Vegetable oil for frying
Sea salt and freshly ground black pepper

Bring the potatoes to the boil in plenty of salted water, then lower the heat and simmer until tender. Drain well and leave to dry for a few minutes, then return to the pan and mash until smooth. Set aside.

Flake the drained tuna into the mashed potato, mix in the spring onions and parsley, then season with salt, pepper and lemon juice. Divide the mixture into 8 balls, then shape them into cakes and dust lightly with flour.

Heat about 1cm (¹/₂ inch) oil in a large frying pan and fry the cakes over a moderate heat for about 5 minutes per side, until they are crisp and brown.

Serves 4

CRAB CAKES

I adore crabs and will happily while away hours cracking claws and picking at the shell with nothing by my side but a pot of mayonnaise, a lemon and lots of napkins to mop up the mess. But I also love crab cakes. I prefer an uncomplicated recipe, as I think the sweetness of the crab is best appreciated this way. I generally use ready-picked crabmeat but if you want to start from scratch and tackle a whole crab, a 650g (1 pound 7 ounce) boiled crab will yield about 150g (5 ounces) of meat.

*900g (2 pounds) floury potatoes, peeled and
    cut into chunks*
300g (11 ounces) fresh white crabmeat
2 free-range eggs
2 tablespoons sliced spring onions
1 tablespoon chopped dill
About 1 teaspoon lemon juice
100g (2 cups) fresh breadcrumbs
Sunflower or vegetable oil for frying
Sea salt and freshly ground black pepper

Cook the potatoes in plenty of boiling salted water until tender, then drain and leave to dry for a few minutes. Place them in a bowl and mash with a potato masher; they don't need to be completely smooth. Add the crabmeat, eggs, spring onions and dill and mix thoroughly. Season with salt, pepper and lemon juice to taste. Divide the mixture into 8, shape into cakes and then roll them in the breadcrumbs. Chill until firm.

Pour some oil into a frying pan until it is 1cm ($^{1}/_{2}$ inch) deep and place over the heat. When it is hot, add the cakes and fry for about 3 minutes per side, until crisp and golden brown. Remove and drain on kitchen paper. Serve with Mayonnaise (see page 152).

Serves 4

SALMON FISHCAKES WITH BEARNAISE SAUCE

Pretty much every restaurant I worked in during the late Eighties had salmon fishcakes on the menu and they were so popular you couldn't make enough of them. I'd put that down to their being ideal comfort food. This recipe is best made with fresh poached salmon but you could substitute a good canned salmon, or even smoked haddock.

Though Béarnaise Sauce is a traditional partner to steak and chips, fishcakes need a good sharp sauce too and this one is perfect.

1kg (2^1/$_4$ pounds) floury potatoes, peeled and
   cut into chunks
Juice of ^{1}/$_2$ lemon
1kg (2^1/$_4$ pounds) salmon fillet, skinned
   and boned
30g (2 tablespoons) unsalted butter, melted
2 tablespoons chopped parsley
2 free-range eggs
50g (^{1}/$_3$ cup) plain flour
150g (3 cups) fresh breadcrumbs
Sunflower oil for deep-frying
Sea salt and freshly ground black pepper
Béarnaise Sauce (see page 154), to serve

Cook the potatoes in plenty of boiling salted water until tender, then drain and leave to dry for a few minutes. Mash them until smooth and set aside.

Bring a large pan of water to the boil and add the lemon juice. Season the fish with salt and pepper and place it in the pan. Let the water come back to the boil, then turn the heat down low and simmer for 8–10 minutes, until the fish is just cooked through. Transfer the fish to a plate and leave it to cool.

Put the mashed potato into a bowl and flake in the fish. Add the melted butter and parsley, combine well and season to taste. Divide the mixture into 12 and shape into cakes. Cover and chill for an hour.

Now you need 3 bowls. In one, whisk the eggs. In the second, mix the flour with some salt and pepper. Have the breadcrumbs in the third. Dust the fishcakes with the flour, then dip them in the egg and finally in the breadcrumbs, pressing the crumbs on well so they stick.

Heat some oil to 180°C/350°F in a deep-fat fryer or deep saucepan and fry the fishcakes in batches for 4–5 minutes, until crisp and golden. Drain on kitchen paper and serve immediately, with the Béarnaise Sauce.

Serves 6

FISH IN BEER BATTER WITH CHIPS

Just like the next person, I'm a sucker for good fish and chips. I love the crisp batter with a succulent fillet of fish sealed inside and first-rate hot, salty chips spiked with lemon. I like to use a beer batter for fish, as it produces a light, crisp coating with the slightly sharp flavour of hops. My favourite varieties for frying are cod, plaice and haddock, but pollock and whiting are also good.

There are a few basic rules to follow when frying fish. First of all, you must have clean oil and lots of it; the fillets need plenty of space to fry in so they don't stick together. The temperature is important, too. Heat the oil to 180–195°C/350–390°F, depending on the thickness of the fillet. Larger chunks of fish should be fried at the lower temperature so the heat of the oil cooks them through without burning the batter. On the other hand, thin fillets should be cooked on the higher heat to crisp up quickly.

I've included two batter recipes below: a traditional yeasted beer batter, which gives a thicker coating to the fish, and a quick, light, lacy beer batter.

Sunflower oil for deep-frying
4 x 175g (6-ounce) white fish fillets, skinned
Sea salt and freshly ground black pepper

For a traditional beer batter
10g (¹/₃ ounce) fresh yeast or 5g (1 teaspoon)
  dried yeast
¹/₂ teaspoon sugar
200ml (scant 1 cup) beer
140g (scant 1 cup) plain flour
¹/₂ teaspoon sea salt

For a light beer batter
150g (1 cup) self-raising flour
¹/₂ teaspoon sea salt
200ml (scant 1 cup) ice-cold beer

To serve
Chips (page 147)
Mushy Peas (page 156), if liked

If you are making the traditional beer batter, put the yeast and sugar in a bowl and stir in enough of the beer to make a smooth paste, then stir in the rest of the beer. Sift in the flour and salt and whisk into a batter. Leave it to rest for at least an hour before using.

If you are making the light batter, sift the flour and salt into a bowl, pour in the beer and mix together quickly. It will be a little lumpy, but that's okay; the lumps will pop in the oil to make crispy scraps. Use immediately.

Heat the oil in a deep-fat fryer or deep saucepan to 180–195°C/350–390°F, depending on the thickness of the fish fillets. Season the fillets with salt and pepper and dip them into the batter. It's best to cook them in batches, so as not to crowd the pan. Carefully lower the fish into the hot oil and fry for about 6–8 minutes, depending on size, until golden brown and crisp. Drain on kitchen paper and keep warm in a low oven while you fry the rest of the fish. Serve with chips, and with Mushy Peas, if you like.

Serves 4

FILLETS OF SOLE ST GERMAIN

A French classic and one of the first fish dishes I learned at college. At the time I thought it was unnecessarily fussy – all the tricky filleting, trying hard not to singe the delicate fish fillets while keeping an eye on the potatoes, hoping that the butter didn't burn. But in fact it is really a very easy dish to prepare. Have the potatoes ready so you can turn your full attention to the fish.

150g (²/₃ cup) unsalted butter
50g (¹/₃ cup) plain flour
150g (3 cups) fresh breadcrumbs
12 lemon sole fillets
600g (1¹/₄ pounds) small new potatoes,
  scraped and cut into quarters
Sea salt and freshly ground black pepper
Béarnaise Sauce (see page 154), to serve

Melt the butter in a large frying pan and pour half of it into a bowl. Season the flour with salt and pepper and put it in a large, shallow bowl. Put the breadcrumbs in another bowl. Dip the sole fillets into the flour and shake off the excess. Dip them into the melted butter and then press them firmly into the breadcrumbs until coated on both sides.

Put the frying pan back on the heat. When the butter is hot, add the diced potatoes and cook over a medium heat, stirring occasionally, until they are soft and golden. Season with salt and pepper.

Grill the sole fillets under a medium heat, being careful not to singe the breadcrumbs. They should take 3–4 minutes per side. Arrange the sole fillets on 6 warm plates, surrounded by the potatoes, and serve the Béarnaise Sauce on the side.

Serves 6

PLAICE FILLETS IN A PARMESAN CRUST

It's no wonder that plaice is a fish-and-chip-shop favourite. The thin, flat fillets are quick to cook and perfect for deep-frying. Instead of battering the fish, though, try encasing it in a shield of breadcrumbs. I like to add a little Parmesan to the crumbs. It gives the crust a slightly salty boost – a perfect complement to the natural sweetness of plaice. Serve this with a bowl of chips and wedges of lemon.

50g (¹/₃ cup) plain flour
2 free-range eggs, lightly beaten
100g (2 cups) breadcrumbs, made from
  day-old bread
50g (¹/₂ cup) Parmesan cheese, finely grated
4 x 175g (6-ounce) plaice fillets, skinned
Sunflower oil for deep-frying
Sea salt and freshly ground black pepper

To serve
Lemon wedges
Chips (see page 147)
Tartare Sauce (see page 152)

Put the flour in a large shallow dish, the eggs in another and the breadcrumbs and Parmesan in a third. Season the plaice fillets on each side with salt and pepper and dust them with flour, shaking off the excess. Dip them in the egg, then toss with the combined breadcrumbs and Parmesan, pressing the crumbs lightly on to the flesh to get an even coating.

Heat some oil to 190°C/375°F in a deep-fat fryer or a deep saucepan and fry the fish, in batches if necessary, for 2–3 minutes, until crisp and golden. Drain on kitchen paper and serve immediately, with lemon wedges, chips and Tartare Sauce.

Serves 4

MATZO-CRUMBED WHITING WITH POTATO LATKES

I suppose this is fish and chips, Yiddish style. Latkes are one of the most famous Jewish foods and are a speciality of Hanukkah, the festival of lights, though they are eaten all year round, often served as a starter with dips and pickled fish. There are many variations on latkes, both sweet and savoury, but potato ones are by far the most popular. Matzo meal gives a lighter coating to the fish than regular breadcrumbs. It is available in some delicatessens and supermarkets.

150g (1 cup) matzo meal
1 free-range egg, beaten with 1 tablespoon
    milk
50g (⅓ cup) plain flour
12 x 80g (3-ounce) whiting fillets, skinned
Sea salt and freshly ground black pepper
Tartare Sauce (see page 152), to serve

For the latkes
1kg (2¼ pounds) waxy potatoes
1 small onion
1 tablespoon plain flour
2 tablespoons chopped parsley
1 free-range egg, lightly beaten
Sunflower oil for frying

First make the latkes. Peel the potatoes and coarsely grate them into a bowl. Cover them with cold water and let them soak for 10 minutes to extract the starch. Drain the potatoes and squeeze out the excess moisture. Coarsely grate the onion into a clean bowl and add the potato. Mix in the flour, parsley and egg and stir until well combined. Season with salt and pepper.

Heat about 2cm (¾ inch) sunflower oil in a frying pan. With wet hands, shape the potato mixture into 12 flat cakes and fry them in batches over a medium heat for about 2 minutes on each side, until they are crisp and brown. Remove from the pan with a fish slice, drain on kitchen paper and keep warm in a low oven.

Put the matzo meal in a shallow bowl and season with salt and pepper. Put the egg and milk in another bowl and the flour in a third. Lightly season the fish fillets, then dust them with the flour, shaking off any excess. Coat the fillets in the egg mixture and then in the matzo meal, pressing it on lightly so the fish is completely covered.

Heat the oil again in the frying pan to 2cm (¾ inch) depth, topping it up with more oil if necessary, then fry the fish fillets in batches over a medium heat for about 3 minutes on each side, until golden and cooked through. Drain and keep warm with the latkes in the oven until all of the fish is done.

Divide the fish and latkes between 6 warmed plates and serve with the Tartare Sauce and a green salad.

Serves 6

MUSSEL CROQUETTES

These mussel-spiked croquettes can be made in minuscule size to be handed around with drinks at a party or as larger cakes to be served with vegetables or a salad as a main meal.

1kg (2¹/₄ pounds) mussels
125ml (¹/₂ cup) white wine
1kg (2¹/₄ pounds) floury potatoes, peeled and
*   cut into chunks*
6 spring onions, finely sliced
3 free-range eggs
Plain flour for dusting
100g (2 cups) fresh breadcrumbs
Sunflower or vegetable oil for frying
Sea salt and freshly ground black pepper

Scrub the mussels to remove any sand or barnacles and pull out their beards – the hairy bit poking out of the shell. Tap any open mussels on the work surface to see if they close; discard them if they don't. Tip the mussels into a large pan and pour in the wine. Cover the pan and place over a high heat. Steam the mussels for about 4–5 minutes, until all of the shells have opened. Drain the mussels, pull them from their shells and chop roughly.

Cook the potatoes in plenty of boiling salted water until tender, then drain and leave to dry for a few minutes. Mash well in a bowl and combine with the mussels and spring onions. Beat in 2 of the eggs and season with salt and pepper.

Flour your hands and shape the mixture into little sausage shapes or larger cakes. Put some flour in one shallow dish, beat the remaining egg in another, and put the breadcrumbs in a third. Coat the croquettes lightly in flour, dip them in the egg, then roll them in the breadcrumbs. Chill for an hour, until firm.

Pour some oil into a frying pan until it is about 5cm (2 inches) deep. Add the croquettes and fry for 2–3 minutes, until golden brown. Drain on kitchen paper and serve piping hot, with Mayonnaise (see page 152).

Makes about 24 small croquettes, 8 large ones

SCAMPI AND STRAW POTATOES

This recipe is inspired by a main course from the great Harry's Bar in Venice, which is also always on the menu of its sister restaurants, Cipriani in London and New York. Scampi is the Italian word for langoustine or Dublin Bay prawns, though you could use king prawns instead. It's just posh scampi and chips, really.

800g (1³/₄ pounds) waxy potatoes
1kg (2¹/₄ pounds) good-sized raw
  langoustines
Sunflower oil for deep-frying
50g (¹/₃ cup) plain flour
Sea salt and freshly ground black pepper
Tartare Sauce (see page 152), to serve

Peel the potatoes and slice them into long strips about the width of a matchstick. Rinse them in plenty of cold water, dry thoroughly with a tea towel and set aside.

Now peel the langoustines. Pull the heads off – this is the difficult bit, as the shell is hard and spiky – then hold each one in a tea towel and press the shell together, cracking the underside between their little legs. If you pull the legs back, the shell should come apart, then you can peel if off as you would for a prawn. I keep the heads and shells to make stock.

Heat the oil to 180°C/350°F in a deep-fat fryer or a deep saucepan. Plunge the potatoes into the oil and cook for 4–5 minutes, until they are golden brown (you will need to do this in batches). Remove and drain on kitchen paper, then season with salt and pepper. Keep warm in a low oven.

Put the flour in a shallow bowl and season with salt and pepper. Pass the langoustines through it, shaking off any excess. Fry them in the hot oil, in batches, for about 1 minute, until they become a rosy pink. Remove and drain on kitchen paper.

Arrange the langoustines around the outside of 4 plates and place a handful of the straw potatoes in the middle. Serve with the Tartare Sauce and a green salad.

Serves 4

SALT COD TORTILLA

You'll find tortilla amongst the tapas in every bar or café in Spain, eaten hot or cold, a thick wedge shoved into a *bocadillo* or between a couple of slices of bread for lunch. The name tortilla is derived from the word *torta*, meaning tart or cake, but it is more like a large omelette, made with sweet stewed onions and potatoes. Sometimes it also includes spinach, roasted peppers, young asparagus tips or peas, though here this omelette contains Spain's best-loved fish, salt cod.

300g (11 ounces) salt cod, soaked for
    12 hours or overnight in several changes
    of water
200ml (scant 1 cup) olive oil
2 onions, sliced
800g (1³/₄ pounds) waxy potatoes,
    peeled and cut into slices about 5mm
    (¹/₄ inch) thick
8 free-range eggs
2 tablespoons chopped parsley
Sea salt and freshly ground black pepper

Drain the salt cod and put it in a large pan of fresh water. Bring to the boil and simmer for 20 minutes, until it is beginning to flake from the bone. Drain and set aside to cool a little, then peel off the skin and discard the bones. Flake the fish while it is still warm, as when it cools it can become too tough and sticky to prise apart easily.

Heat half the oil in a large, heavy-based frying pan until almost smoking hot, then stir in the onions and a pinch of salt. Turn the heat down and cook for 20 minutes, until soft and golden brown. Remove from the pan with a slotted spoon and set aside.

Heat the rest of the oil in the pan, add the potatoes and fry over a medium heat for about 10–15 minutes, stirring every few minutes, until they are crisp and brown.

Drain the potatoes and reserve the cooking oil. In a bowl, beat the eggs lightly and add the onions, fish, potatoes and parsley. Season with a grind of pepper and check for salt; it may need a little.

Heat the reserved oil in the pan until hot, then pour in the tortilla mixture with one hand and shake the pan with the other; this will help to stop it sticking. Reduce the heat and cook for about 5 minutes, until the underneath is set and the mixture is coming away from the sides of the pan. To turn the tortilla, put a large plate over the top and invert the pan so the tortilla rests on the plate. Watch out, as it will be a bit runny. Slide the tortilla back into the pan and continue to cook for 5 minutes or until set underneath. It should feel solid in the middle but if it doesn't, place it in a moderate oven until firm. If this all seems a bit tricky, then rather than turning the tortilla you can just place it under a medium grill until set on top. To serve, turn the omelette out and cut it into wedges.

Serves 4-6

GRILLED

GRILLED LOBSTER WITH HERB BUTTER AND CHIPS

This is a superb way of preparing lobsters. What I really love about this dish is the sweet, buttery juices that seep from the shells, perfect to squish your chips into as you mop every last bit of juice from the plate.

5 litres (5 quarts) water
200g ($^3/_4$ cup) sea salt
2 lobsters, weighing about 800g
  (1$^3/_4$ pounds) each
60g (4 tablespoons) unsalted butter
1 teaspoon chopped parsley
1 teaspoon chopped chives
1 tablespoon lemon juice
Sea salt and freshly ground black pepper
Chips (see page 147), to serve

Put the water and salt in a large pot and bring to a rolling boil. Plunge the lobsters head first into the water and cover the pot to bring it back to the boil quickly. Simmer for 5 minutes, then remove the lobsters from the water and leave until cool enough to handle. Meanwhile, melt the butter in a pan and remove from the heat.

Preheat the grill. Place the lobsters on a chopping board and cut through the middle of the head with a large, heavy knife, bringing it down between the eyes. Turn the lobster around and then cut right through the middle of the tail to split it in half. Crack opens the claws with the back of the knife, using the heavy end near the handle. Remove the intestinal thread running through the back of the lobster and the bony sac inside the head. Place the lobster halves on a grill tray, flesh-side up, brush them with a little of the melted butter and grill under a medium heat for 8–10 minutes, until the flesh is firm and lightly golden on top.

Warm the butter a little and add the chopped herbs. Season with salt and pepper and the lemon juice. Transfer the lobster to 4 warm plates and spoon over the herby butter. Serve with chips (or new potatoes) and a green salad.

Serves 4

GRILLED SWORDFISH WITH POTATOES AND SALMORIGLIO

Salmoriglio is a southern Italian sauce used predominantly with fish. As swordfish is native to that area, this is the first fish I would choose to serve it with, though tuna would be a fair substitute. Salmoriglio can be rather overpowering, since it's mostly made with oregano, sometimes with marjoram. My version uses equal quantities of oregano and parsley for a milder flavour.

1kg (2^1/$_4$ pounds) waxy new potatoes, scrubbed
6 x 175g (6-ounce) swordfish steaks
A little olive oil
Sea salt and freshly ground black pepper

For the salmoriglio
50g (1 cup) fresh oregano
50g (1 cup) flat-leaf parsley
1 garlic clove, peeled
Juice of 1 lemon
^{1}/$_2$ teaspoon sea salt
100ml (scant ^{1}/$_2$ cup) olive oil

For the salmoriglio, put the herbs, garlic, lemon juice and salt in a food processor and process, gradually adding the olive oil until emulsified. Set aside.

Put the potatoes in a pan of salted water and bring to the boil. Simmer until tender, then drain and leave until cool enough to handle. Slice the potatoes into discs and toss with a little of the salmoriglio.

Preheat a ridged grill pan until it is smoking. Season the fish with salt and pepper and rub with a little extra olive oil. Place on the hot grill and cook for 1–2 minutes on each side. It should be medium rare – always best for swordfish. Well-done swordfish can be dry and rather unpleasant.

Transfer the fish to serving plates, spoon over a little salmoriglio and pile the potatoes alongside.

Serves 6

GRILLED OCTOPUS WITH FRIED POTATOES

I encountered this dish while holidaying on the Greek island of Santorini some years ago. I ate it for lunch pretty much every day and pestered the chef until she gave me the recipe. It was worth persevering, as I still regularly make it today.

Greek cooks prefer the heady flavour of dried oregano to fresh and never skin the octopus, believing that the skin adds flavour and texture to a dish. I firmly agree.

2–3 small octopus, weighing about 1.2kg
(2^3/$_4$ pounds) in total
800g (1^3/$_4$ pounds) waxy potatoes
150ml (^{2}/$_3$ cup) extra virgin olive oil
2 teaspoons dried oregano
Juice of 1 lemon
4 garlic cloves, finely sliced
Sea salt and freshly ground black pepper

Clean the octopus by slicing the tentacles away from the head, just under the hard beak, below the eyes. Turn the body inside out and remove the innards. Rub the head and tentacles with salt to help dislodge any sand or grit, then rinse under cold running water.

Bring a large pan of water to the boil, add the octopus body and tentacles, then reduce the heat. Simmer gently for about 40 minutes, until tender, then drain. Slice into 2cm (^{3}/$_4$ inch) pieces.

Meanwhile, boil the potatoes in their skins until tender, then drain and set aside. When they are cool enough to handle, peel them and slice into 2cm (^{3}/$_4$ inch) discs.

Cook the octopus in 50ml (3^1/$_2$ tablespoons) of the olive oil in a heavy-based frying pan over a high heat for about 5 minutes, until charred, then transfer to a bowl. Toss with 50ml (3^1/$_2$ tablespoons) of the remaining olive oil, plus the oregano and lemon juice.

Heat the remaining oil in the pan, add the potato slices and fry over a medium heat until browned on both sides. Add the garlic and stir around until it becomes golden.

Toss the potatoes with the octopus and season with salt and pepper. Serve with crusty bread and black olives.

Serves 6

CHERMOULA MACKEREL WITH NEW POTATO, YOGHURT AND CORIANDER SALAD

Chermoula is a delicious, powerfully flavoured marinade used with fish all over North Africa. It goes with almost any type of fish – I think that mackerel, being a strong oily fish, copes with the strength of the spices beautifully. Be sure to grill it over a medium heat, otherwise the spices can burn and become bitter.

4 large mackerel, weighing about 300–350g (11–12 ounces) each
1 quantity of Chermoula (see page 153)
1 lime, quartered

For the salad
800g (1³/4 pounds) waxy new potatoes, scrubbed
250g (1 cup) Greek-style yoghurt
1 tablespoon tahini
2 teaspoons honey
1 teaspoon ground cumin
1 small red onion, finely sliced
1–2 green chillies, seeded and finely sliced
A small bunch of coriander, chopped
Sea salt and freshly ground black pepper

Carefully slash the skin of the mackerel on both sides at 1cm (¹/2 inch) intervals all the way down the fish, taking care not to cut too deeply into the flesh. Rub the chermoula paste on to the fish, massaging it lightly into the cuts and the cavity. Leave to marinate while you make the potato salad.

Cook the potatoes in boiling salted water until tender, then drain and set aside to cool a little. In a bowl, whisk together the yoghurt, tahini, honey and cumin until well combined and season with salt and pepper to taste. Slice the still-warm potatoes into discs and add to the dressing; they will absorb the flavours more readily while they are warm. Mix in the onion, chilli and coriander.

Preheat a ridged grill pan or a barbecue. Place the fish on the grill and cook for 3 minutes on each side. Squeeze the lime over the fish before taking it off the grill. Transfer to serving plates, with the potato salad on the side.

Serves 4

GRILLED SARDINES WITH POTATOES, SPINACH, PINE NUTS AND RAISINS

Grilled sardines are a classic, especially outdoors on the barbecue. The Moorish-influenced combination of spinach, pine nuts and raisins is traditional to the Catalan region of Spain. I add potatoes to this dish to make it more substantial. It is equally good hot or cold.

500g (1 pound 2 ounces) waxy potatoes
3 tablespoons olive oil
30g ($^{1}/_{4}$ cup) pine nuts
1 garlic clove, finely chopped
30g ($2^{1}/_{2}$ tablespoons) raisins, soaked in hot
    water for 1 hour, then drained
4 anchovy fillets
1kg ($2^{1}/_{4}$ pounds) fresh spinach
Juice of 1 lemon, plus lemon wedges to
    serve
24 sardines, scaled and gutted (you could
    ask your fishmonger to do this)
Sea salt and freshly ground black pepper

Cook the potatoes in their skins in plenty of boiling salted water until tender, then drain. When they are cool enough to handle, peel them and cut into 1cm ($^{1}/_{2}$ inch) dice.

Heat a wok or large frying pan, add 2 tablespoons of the olive oil and heat until almost smoking. Add the potatoes and fry until brown all over. Add the pine nuts and garlic and cook until they take on a golden colour. Stir in the drained raisins and the anchovies and cook for 30 seconds. Add the spinach and toss until it starts to wilt, then season with salt and pepper and the lemon juice. Pile the mixture on to a platter.

Preheat a ridged grill pan or a barbecue. Season the sardines with salt and pepper and rub them with the remaining olive oil.

Carefully place the sardines on the grill and cook for about 2 minutes. Don't try to move them until they are coming away from the grill, then flip them over and cook for a further 2 minutes. Transfer to a warm platter and serve with the potato mixture and lemon wedges on the side.

Serves 6

BARBECUED GREY MULLET WITH SWEET POTATO AND PRESERVED LEMON SALAD

I think that grey mullet is the most underrated of fish. In fact, I'd go as far as to saying that a spanking-fresh mullet is equal to sea bass. It's rarely off my menus in the summer months. Good and meaty, with a slightly muddy flavour, it stands up well to the charring of the barbecue.

2 large sweet potatoes (around 1kg/2¹/₄
pounds total weight), peeled and cut into
2cm (³/₄ inch) chunks
100ml (scant ¹/₂ cup) olive oil, plus a little
more for cooking the fish
25ml (2 tablespoons) red wine vinegar
¹/₂ teaspoon sugar
75g (3 ounces) preserved lemons, flesh
scraped out and discarded, rind thinly
sliced
100g (²/₃ cup) black olives
4 grey mullet fillets, weighing about 250g
(9 ounces) each
Sea salt and freshly ground black pepper

Put the sweet potato chunks in a bowl, drizzle with 25ml (2 tablespoons) of the olive oil, then season with salt and pepper and toss to combine. Cook the potatoes on a barbecue or a ridged grill pan over a fairly low heat, turning occasionally, for about 20 minutes or until tender.

Mix together the vinegar, sugar and the rest of the olive oil. Return the potatoes to the bowl and add the preserved lemon rind and olives. Pour over the dressing, toss gently to combine and set aside.

Make a couple of cuts, not too deep, in the skin of each fish fillet (grey mullet skin tends to curl when introduced to the heat). Lightly oil the fish and season it with salt and pepper. Barbecue or grill for 2–3 minutes on each side, until the flesh is firm to the touch. Transfer the fish to plates and serve the salad alongside.

Serves 4

BAKED

HAKE STEAKS BAKED WITH POTATOES

This Portuguese recipe for hake is adapted from Jane Grigson's book, *Fish Cookery* (Penguin, 1973). It has an unusual way of baking the fish topped with mayonnaise, which strangely doesn't split but oozes into the fish and potatoes below, leaving a lovely gooey brown crust on top.

600g (1^1/$_4$ pounds) waxy potatoes
Olive oil for frying
4 x 175g (6-ounce) hake steaks
Juice of ^{1}/$_2$ lemon
1 quantity of Mayonnaise (see page 152),
   made using a mixture of vegetable oil and
   olive oil to taste
1 onion, finely sliced
Sea salt and freshly ground black pepper

Preheat the oven to 180°C/350°F/Gas Mark 4. Boil the potatoes in their skins until they are just tender, then drain. When they are cool enough to handle, peel them and cut into small dice. Heat 1cm (^{1}/$_2$ inch) olive oil in a frying pan, add the potatoes and fry over a medium heat until they are golden brown all over. Season with salt and pepper.

Arrange the hake steaks in a gratin dish in a single layer, season them with salt and pepper and squeeze over the lemon juice. Scatter the potatoes over and around the fish and spoon the mayonnaise on top – for the most part over the fish steaks. Sprinkle with the onion slices and bake for 20–30 minutes, until the fish is cooked and the mayonnaise has browned on top.

Serves 4

SEA BASS EN PAPILLOTE

This is an attractive way of cooking fish fillets. Though it may seem a bit fiddly, it's well worth the effort. The fish steams in the buttery, winey juices and, encased with the potatoes and radicchio, gives you a complete meal in a parcel. It's great for a dinner party – you can make up the parcels beforehand and cook them just as you need them.

600g (1¼ pounds) new potatoes, scrubbed
1 head of radicchio
A little extra virgin olive oil
6 x 175g (6-ounce) sea bass fillets
60g (4 tablespoons) unsalted butter
A glass of white wine
Sea salt and freshly ground black pepper

Cook the potatoes in plenty of boiling salted water until tender, then drain. When they are cool enough to handle, slice them into thin discs. Pull the leaves from the radicchio and set aside.

Preheat the oven to 200°C/400°F/Gas Mark 6. Cut out 6 heart-shaped pieces of greaseproof paper, large enough to envelop the fish. Lightly brush one half of each heart with a little oil and place a couple of leaves of radicchio on it. Place the potatoes on top of the leaves, then top with the fish fillets. Season the fish with salt and pepper and add a knob of the butter and a splash of white wine. Fold over the other half of the paper and seal the edges by turning them over tightly a few turns. Place on a baking tray and bake for 10–12 minutes; the paper will brown and puff up a little.

Transfer the parcels to serving plates, so each guest can open them at the table and breathe in the beautiful aroma.

Serves 6

HERBY SEA BASS WITH MASH

This recipe was given to me by my good friend and fishmonger, Ben Woodcraft. Ben runs his business from Mersea Island off the south coast of Essex, where the fishermen land the most beautiful line-caught bass. He is also a keen cook and often gives me the rundown of the dishes he prepares at home.

You could use fillets of sea bass for this recipe and fry or grill them but I prefer to cook the fish whole in the oven. The less-direct heat and longer cooking time help to keep it moist and succulent.

2 sea bass, weighing about 800g
  (1³/4 pounds) in total, scaled and trimmed
  of their fins
150ml (²/3 cup) extra virgin olive oil
A handful of basil leaves
A handful of parsley
A handful of mint leaves
Juice of 1 lemon
Sea salt and freshly ground black pepper
Mashed Potato (see page 145), to serve

Preheat the oven to its highest setting. Slash the fish to the bone 2 or 3 times on each side near the head end, so that they will cook evenly. Season inside and out with salt and pepper and place in an ovenproof dish. Lubricate the fish with 50ml (3¹/2 tablespoons) of the olive oil and put into the hot oven. Turn the heat down to 200°C/400°F/Gas Mark 6 and bake for about 25 minutes, until the flesh is firm and beginning to flake from the bone.

Meanwhile, chop the herbs roughly and mix them with the remaining olive oil and lemon juice to taste. Season with salt and pepper. To serve, place a large dollop of the mashed potato on to warmed plates, carefully lift the fish fillets away from the backbone and lay them next to the mash. Pass the green sauce around separately.

Serves 4

BAKED BREAM (BESUGO AL HORNO)

This traditional Spanish way of cooking bream is found in just about every fine restaurant in Spain. A *besugo* is a wood-fired open brick oven built into the restaurant wall, often visible from outside the restaurant. There a whole fish would be cooked in a *cazuela* – an earthenware dish that can be used on top of the stove as well as in the oven and then taken directly to the table.

750g (1 pound 10 ounces) waxy potatoes, peeled and cut into slices 2cm ($^3/_4$ inch) thick
250ml (1 cup) olive oil
2 large onions, sliced
1 sea bream, weighing about 2kg ($4^1/_2$ pounds), cleaned and scaled
1 lemon, sliced, plus lemon wedges to serve
3 garlic cloves, sliced
8 tablespoons fresh breadcrumbs
2 tablespoons chopped parsley
Sea salt and freshly ground black pepper

Preheat the oven to 220°C/425°F/Gas Mark 7. Cook the potato slices in a pan of boiling salted water until they are half done, then drain.

Heat 50ml ($3^1/_2$ tablespoons) of the olive oil in a frying pan, add the onions and sauté until they are soft and translucent. Add the potatoes and stir to coat them with the oil. Transfer the mixture to a gratin dish large enough to hold the bream.

Make 2 or 3 slashes through to the bone on each side of the fish, at the plump end close to the head. Season the fish inside and out with salt and pepper and push the lemon slices into the cavity. Put the fish on top of the potatoes and onions.

Heat the remaining olive oil in the pan, add the garlic and fry until golden and fragrant. Mix in the breadcrumbs and parsley, then spread the mixture over the bream. Bake for 30–40 minutes, until the fish is done. If it is browning too quickly, cover with foil. Serve with lemon wedges, a green salad and a bottle or two of rosé.

Serves 6

JOHN DORY WITH POTATOES, GARLIC AND CREAM

This is essentially a creamy, fishy gratin, based on the great gratin dauphinois. You need good thick fillets of fish here, and John Dory has the firm texture and essential sweetness to take on the richness of all that garlic and cream. It makes a wonderful supper with just a simple salad.

200ml (scant 1 cup) milk
200ml (scant 1 cup) double cream
1.2kg (2³/4 pounds) waxy potatoes, peeled and thinly sliced
6 garlic cloves, finely sliced
60g (4 tablespoons) unsalted butter
4 x 175g (6-ounce) John Dory fillets
Sea salt and freshly ground black pepper

Preheat the oven to 180°C/350°F/Gas Mark 4. In a large pan, heat the milk until it only just comes to the boil, then remove the pan from the stove and stir in the cream. Season with salt and pepper, add the potatoes and garlic and stir about to coat them well.

Spread most of the butter around the inside of a gratin dish, leaving a little to dot on top of the gratin. Layer the potato slices in the dish, overlapping them a little, then pour over the cream and milk mixture. Cover the dish with foil and bake for about 50 minutes, until the potatoes are almost done.

Season the fish with salt and pepper, remove the foil from the baking dish and place the fillets on top of the potato. Return to the oven and bake for 10–12 minutes, until the fish is cooked.

Serves 4

RED MULLET WITH BLACK OLIVES AND POTATOES

A dish of Greek origin. Locally, small red mullet, or barbounia, as they are known there, would be used. Sweet as they are, the little ones tend to be bony and a bit fiddly, so I've used larger fish here.

100ml (scant ¹/₂ cup) olive oil, plus extra
    for drizzling
1 red onion, finely chopped
2 garlic cloves, chopped
1kg (2¹/₄ pounds) waxy potatoes, peeled and
    cut into 2cm (³/₄ inch) dice
2 tomatoes, skinned and chopped
250ml (1 cup) white wine
2 large red mullet, weighing about 750g
    (1 pound 10 ounces) each, cleaned
    and scaled
100g (²/₃ cup) black olives
Salt and freshly ground black pepper

Preheat the oven to 220°C/425°F/Gas Mark 7. Heat the olive oil in a large frying pan, add the onion and garlic and cook over a low heat until soft. Add the potatoes and stir to coat them in the oil, then stir in the tomatoes and white wine. Cover and stew gently until the potatoes are tender. Season with salt and pepper and transfer the mixture to a gratin dish large enough to hold the fish.

Make 2 or 3 slashes through to the bone on each side of the fish, at the plump end near the head. Season the fish inside and out and place on top of the potato mixture. Scatter the olives around and drizzle over a little extra olive oil. Bake for 20–30 minutes, until the fish is done. Serve with salad and crusty bread.

Serves 4

STUFFED SQUID BAKED WITH POTATOES AND ONIONS

Squid is a versatile little beast, as happy to be baked or deep-fried as it is to be braised or grilled. It is perhaps most popular as *calamari* – sliced into neat little rings, crumbed or battered, then fried until crisp, the perfect finger food.

This recipe uses whole squid, the perfect pocket-shaped vessel crying out to be stuffed with a variety of fillings. Squid stuffed and baked in this way hails from southern Italy.

6 medium squid (about 12cm/5 inches long)
    or 12 small squid
500g (1 pound 2 ounces) waxy new potatoes,
    cut in half
500g (1 pound 2 ounces) red onions, peeled
    and cut into eighths with the root still
    attached
125ml (¹/₂ cup) olive oil
200ml (scant 1 cup) white wine
Sea salt and freshly ground black pepper
Lemon wedges, to serve

For the stuffing
3 tablespoons olive oil
1 onion, finely chopped
2 garlic cloves, finely chopped
50g (¹/₃ cup) raisins
125g (2¹/₂ cups) fresh breadcrumbs
50g (¹/₂ cup) Pecorino cheese, grated
A pinch or so of dried chilli flakes
1 teaspoon dried oregano
2 tablespoons chopped parsley
1 free-range egg, beaten

To clean the squid, hold the body in one hand and the tentacles in the other. Gently pull and twist and the head and tentacles will come away with the innards. Cut the tentacles away from the head, squeeze out the hard beak, then cut it off and discard it.

Discard the head and innards. Pull away the purple membrane covering the squid and slice off the 'wings', then remove the quill (which looks like a piece of transparent plastic) from inside the body. Wash the squid thoroughly under cold running water and drain.

For the stuffing, chop the squid 'wings' and tentacles finely and place in a bowl. Heat the olive oil in a pan, add the onion and garlic and cook over a medium heat for 5 minutes or so, until the onion is soft and translucent. Transfer to the bowl with the squid and add the raisins, breadcrumbs, Pecorino, chilli and herbs. Mix in the egg and season with salt and pepper. Stuff each squid tube about three-quarters full with the mixture and secure the ends with a wooden toothpick.

Preheat the oven to 180°C/350°F/Gas Mark 4. Lay the potatoes, red onions and squid in a single layer in a gratin dish and pour over the olive oil. Shake the dish around lightly to coat the whole lot in the oil and season with salt and pepper. Now pour in the wine, cover the dish tightly with foil and bake for 1¹/₂ hours, until the vegetables are done and the squid is tender. Serve with the lemon wedges on the side.

Serves 6

SMOKED MACKEREL AND POTATO GRATIN

This recipe comes courtesy of Samantha Waterhouse, my colleague at the Fox, and it's something we make regularly in the colder months. I find it's the perfect supper dish: the beauty of it is that it's so easy to prepare – just 10 minutes' work – then you can pop it in the oven and virtually forget about it for the next hour, to be rewarded with a decadent, smoky, creamy gratin. I suggest serving it with a salad of bitter leaves – frisée, chicory or maybe watercress.

20g (4 teaspoons) unsalted butter
250g (9 ounces) smoked mackerel
1 small white onion, sliced as thinly
  as possible
500g (1 pound 2 ounces) waxy potatoes,
  peeled and cut into slices 5mm ($^1/_4$ inch)
  thick
250ml (1 cup) milk
250ml (1 cup) double cream
2 tablespoons Dijon mustard
Sea salt and freshly ground black pepper

Preheat the oven to 180°C/350°F/Gas Mark 4. Grease a 20cm (8-inch) gratin dish with the butter. Skin the mackerel and flake the flesh into bite-sized chunks, discarding any bones. In a bowl, gently mix together the fish, onion and potatoes and then put them in the gratin dish.

Mix together the milk, cream and mustard, season with salt and pepper and pour it over the potatoes. Cover the dish with foil and bake for 45 minutes. Remove the foil and continue to cook for 10–15 minutes, until the top of the gratin is golden brown, the cream is bubbling and the potatoes are tender.

Serves 4

JANSSON'S TEMPTATION

Probably the most famous dish to come out of Sweden – if you exclude the meatballs and hotdogs at Ikea, that is. There are a couple of stories behind the name Jansson. He was either Erik, a religious fanatic whose only sensual pleasure was eating this rich, creamy gratin, or Adolph, an opera singer who would cook this as a supper for his friends and followers after performances. Whatever the myth, it is a delicious savoury gratin and something I make regularly. It goes well with meat, especially lamb, or makes a light lunch with bread and a green salad.

50g (3 1/2 tablespoons) unsalted butter
2 onions, sliced
2 garlic cloves, finely sliced
1.2kg (2 3/4 pounds) large waxy potatoes, peeled and cut into slices 5mm (1/4 inch) thick
300ml (1 1/4 cups) milk
300ml (1 1/4 cups) double cream
75g (3 ounces) anchovies in oil
Sea salt and freshly ground black pepper

Preheat the oven to 190°C/375°F/Gas Mark 5. Grease a large baking dish with 20g (4 teaspoons) of the butter. Melt the remaining butter in a large pan, add the onions and garlic and sauté until soft and translucent. Add the potatoes and stir in the milk and cream. Tip in the anchovies and their oil and mix everything together so the anchovies are evenly distributed. Season with a little sea salt (remember that the anchovies are salty) and some black pepper.

Pour the whole lot into the baking dish and bake for an hour or until the potatoes are tender. If the top is browning too quickly, cover the dish with foil.

Serves 4 as a substantial lunch, 10 as a side dish

FISH PIE

I always think of fish pie as the classic 'English bistro' dish. Simple, comforting and hugely popular, it's the perfect meal for getting non-fish eaters into eating fish, and that probably comes down to the creamy mashed potato topping. The fish pie I prefer is a fairly basic one – not crammed full of random little pieces of fish, just the one type and preferably cod or pollock. Having said that, I do sometimes add a few prawns if I have them to hand. And the pie needs to be creamy, so try to have your sauce at the consistency where it will just coat the filling, then it will be well flavoured and you won't have the fish swimming around in a sea of juice.

600ml (2^1/$_2$ cups) milk, plus a little extra
    for the mash
100ml (scant ^{1}/$_2$ cup) double cream
800g (1^3/$_4$ pounds) cod (or pollock) fillet
1 bay leaf
6 free-range eggs
100g (7 tablespoons) unsalted butter
50g (^{1}/$_3$ cup) plain flour
A small bunch of parsley, chopped
1.3kg (3 pounds) floury potatoes, peeled and
    cut into chunks
Sea salt and freshly ground black pepper

Pour the milk and cream into a large pan, add the fish and the bay leaf and bring just to the boil. Simmer for 8 minutes, then strain the liquid into a jug and keep warm. Lift the fish out of the pan and leave it to drain on a plate. When it is cool enough to handle, flake the flesh into large chunks and discard the skin and bones.

Boil the eggs for 8 minutes, then drain and cool under cold running water. Peel and cut into thick slices, then set aside.

Melt half the butter in a pan and stir in the flour. Cook gently for 1 minute and then take off the heat. Gradually mix in the warm fishy milk, stirring all the time so it doesn't become lumpy. Return the pan to the heat and simmer gently for 10 minutes, until the sauce has thickened. Remove from the heat, stir in the fish, eggs and chopped parsley and season with salt and pepper.

Preheat the oven to 200°C/400°F/Gas Mark 6. Cook the potatoes in plenty of boiling salted water until tender, then drain well. Mash with the rest of the butter and a little milk to make a smooth and easily spreadable topping. Season to taste.

Pour the fish mixture into a baking dish and cover with the mashed potatoes. Bake for 30–40 minutes, until bubbling hot and golden brown.

Serves 4

SALMON, POTATO AND RICOTTA PIE

This is more like salmon en croûte or a great big pasty than a traditional fish pie. It's quite an impressive dish to present whole to guests at a dinner party, and even better served cold at a picnic. In fact, I would recommend that it is only served cold or at room temperature, rather than straight from the oven, as its quiche-like consistency means it only becomes sliceable as it cools.

50g (3¹/₂ tablespoons) unsalted butter
2 large leeks, sliced
600g (1¹/₄ pounds) waxy potatoes, peeled
    and cut into small dice
350g (1¹/₂ cups) Ricotta cheese
2 free-range eggs
500g (1 pound 2 ounces) salmon fillet,
    skinned and any bones removed
750g (1 pound 10 ounces) puff pastry
1 free-range egg, beaten with a dash of milk,
    to glaze
Sea salt and freshly ground black pepper

Melt the butter in a pan, add the leeks and a pinch of sea salt, then cover and cook over a low heat for 5 minutes or until soft. Add the diced potatoes and cook for 6–7 minutes, until the potatoes are nearly done. Remove from the heat and cool a little.

Place the ricotta and eggs in a bowl and mix until smooth. Season well with salt and pepper. Roughly chop the salmon and add to the ricotta with the leek and potato mixture. Cut the pastry in half and roll out one piece on a lightly floured surface into a rectangle about 20 x 30cm (8 x 12 inches). Roll the other piece of pastry to a rectangle 5cm (2 inches) wider all around than the first.

Lay the smaller pastry rectangle on a lightly greased baking tray and spoon the salmon and ricotta mixture into the middle. Brush the edges with a little of the egg wash and lay the second piece of pastry on top. Press the edges together with a fork and trim away the excess pastry, leaving a 2cm (³/₄ inch) band around the outside. Cut 3 or 4 small vents in the top of the pie and chill for 1 hour.

Preheat the oven to 220°C/425°F/Gas Mark 7. Brush the pie all over with the remaining egg wash and bake for 35–40 minutes, until the pastry is crisp and brown.

Serves 6

EMPANADAS WITH TOMATO SALSA

Empanadas are eaten the length and breadth of Latin America, with recipes differing in every country. This is an adaptation of Argentinean empanadas, though in Argentina they would almost certainly be made with beef. I use a meaty white fish, such as monkfish or coley, or even salmon. They freeze well.

3 tablespoons olive oil
2 red onions, finely chopped
1 garlic clove, finely chopped
$^1/_2$ teaspoon ground cumin
$^1/_2$ teaspoon dried oregano
200g (7 ounces) waxy potatoes, peeled and
    cut into 1cm ($^1/_2$ inch) dice
300g (11 ounces) fish fillets, skinned and cut
    into 1cm ($^1/_2$ inch) dice
1 red chilli, seeded and chopped
Sea salt and freshly ground black pepper

For the pastry
500g ($3^1/_3$ cups) plain flour
$^1/_2$ teaspoon baking powder
2 teaspoons icing sugar
$^1/_2$ teaspoon sea salt
1 free-range egg, lightly beaten
250ml (1 cup) warm milk, plus a little extra
    milk for brushing
100g (scant $^1/_2$ cup) lard, melted

For the tomato salsa
1 small red onion, finely chopped
1 garlic clove, finely chopped
1 small red chilli, finely chopped
4 ripe tomatoes, seeded and chopped
2 tablespoons chopped coriander
2 tablespoons lime juice

To make the pastry, sift the flour, baking powder, icing sugar and salt into a bowl and make a well in the centre. Add the egg, warm milk and melted lard, mix to a firm dough and divide into 10 balls. Cover and set aside, but don't refrigerate the dough or it will become too hard to work.

For the filling, heat the olive oil in a large saucepan, add the onions, garlic and a pinch of salt, then cover and cook for about 5 minutes, until soft. Add the cumin, oregano and potatoes, mix well and cook for a further 5 minutes. Add the fish and chilli and fold them in gently so as not to break the mixture up too much. Cover and continue to cook for about 5 minutes, until the fish is opaque. Season with salt and pepper and set aside to cool.

Preheat the oven to 200°C/400°F/Gas Mark 6. On a lightly floured board, roll each pastry ball out into a circle about 14cm (6 inches) in diameter. Place some of the fish mixture on one half of the circle and brush the edges with milk. Fold over the pastry to enclose the filling, then crimp the edges to seal.

Place the empanadas on a baking sheet and bake for 10–12 minutes, until browned. Meanwhile, make the salsa. Combine all the ingredients in a bowl, season to taste with sea salt and pepper and leave to stand for 10 minutes for the flavours to develop.

Serve the empanadas hot or at room temperature, accompanied by the salsa.

Makes 10

PIZZA BIANCA

A style of pizza I have eaten in and around Rome, sold in large, crisp slices by street vendors and eaten on the hoof as a mid-morning snack. It is called bianca, or white pizza, because it doesn't contain tomatoes. At home I prefer to have the tomatoes in a salad on the side.

To achieve the best results, your oven needs to be good and hot. I preheat mine on the highest temperature for at least 15 minutes before cooking the pizzas. I use a pizza stone, though a baking tray will do the job well enough. Put your tray in the oven near the top (this should be its hottest point) when you turn it on. This will seal the base of the pizza – the first step to a crisp bottom.

200g (7 ounces) waxy new potatoes, peeled and sliced as thinly as possible
225g (8 ounces) buffalo Mozzarella cheese, chopped
50g (2-ounce) can or jar of anchovies, drained
1 teaspoon chopped rosemary
Olive oil for drizzling

For the dough
500g (3^1/$_2$ cups) strong white flour
1 teaspoon salt
1 sachet (1^1/$_2$ teaspoons) dried Easyblend yeast
^{1}/$_2$ teaspoon sugar
50ml (3^1/$_2$ tablespoons) olive oil, plus a little extra for greasing
250ml (1 cup) warm water

To make the dough, sift the flour and salt into a food processor or an electric mixer fitted with a dough hook, then add the yeast and sugar. Mix the olive oil and water together. Slowly pour the liquid into the food processor or mixer and mix until the dough forms a ball. If it seems too dry, add a little warm water; conversely, if it's wet, add flour by the spoonful until the dough is smooth and elastic. Grease a large bowl with a little olive oil and put the dough in it. Cover with a cloth and leave to rise in a warm place until doubled in size.

Preheat the oven to 250°C/500°F/Gas Mark 10 (or as high as it will go) and put a baking sheet or pizza stone in it near the top.

Cut out 2 large squares of baking parchment. Knock down the dough and divide it in half. Flatten each piece into a round and roll it out as thinly as possible on the baking parchment. Allow the dough to rest for 5 minutes; it will spring back a little.

Press the potato slices gently into the pizza bases and arrange the pieces of Mozzarella over the top. Scatter the anchovies over and sprinkle with the rosemary, then drizzle with a little olive oil. Place one of the pizzas, on its baking parchment, on the hot tray in the oven and bake for 15 minutes, until the potatoes are brown and the Mozzarella bubbling. Repeat with the second pizza. Serve with a salad of plum tomatoes simply dressed with a squeeze of lemon, some sea salt and pepper and a drizzle of olive oil.

Makes 2 x 24cm (10-inch) pizzas

BAKED POTATOES WITH SALMON

This is easy-peasy and makes a wonderful TV dinner. I use canned salmon, though you could use leftover poached salmon, sea trout or even a small amount of smoked salmon. Yum.

4 medium-sized baking potatoes
40g (3 tablespoons) unsalted butter, melted
200g (7 ounces) canned salmon, drained
4 tablespoons crème fraîche
2 spring onions, finely sliced
1 tablespoon chopped dill
1 tablespoon lemon juice
Sea salt and freshly ground black pepper

Preheat the oven to 220°C/425°F/Gas Mark 7. Wash the potatoes and pat them dry. Brush them with the melted butter, sprinkle over some sea salt and wrap each potato in aluminium foil. Bake for about 50 minutes or until tender, then remove from the oven and let them cool a little.

When the potatoes are easy to handle, slice the top off each one and carefully scoop out the flesh, reserving the skins. Mash the flesh in a bowl with a fork until smooth, then mix in the drained salmon, crème fraîche, spring onions and dill. Season with salt and pepper and the lemon juice to taste.

Spoon the filling back into the potato skins and rewrap them in the foil. Return to the oven for about 10 minutes, until heated through, opening the top of the foil after 8 minutes or so to crisp the tops.

Serves 4

FISH PASTIES

Cornish pasties originated as a portable lunch for tin miners, farmers and fishermen to take to work with them. The traditional filling was beef, onion and potato but they would fill them with pretty much any ingredient, and have a jam pasty for pudding. Strangely for a coastal area, fish was deemed inappropriate as a filling. And many a superstitious fisherman refused to take pasties on board their boats when they set off to fish, as they were said to bring bad luck.

I've cheekily adapted this recipe from the man who has put Cornish cooking on the map, Rick Stein. He advises using a cheap fish, such as ling or coley.

100g (3½ ounces) leeks, cut into 1cm
    (½ inch) dice
100g (3½ ounces) onions, cut into 1cm
    (½ inch) dice
225g (8 ounces) potatoes, peeled and cut
    into 1cm (½ inch) dice
450g (1 pound) fish fillet, skinned and cut
    into 2.5cm dice
Juice of ½ lemon
25g (2 tablespoons) unsalted butter
25g (¼ cup) Cheddar cheese, grated
1 teaspoon chopped chives
Sea salt and freshly ground black pepper

For the shortcrust pastry
500g (3⅓ cups) plain flour
A pinch of sea salt
250g (1 cup) unsalted butter, diced
About 5 tablespoons cold water (enough
    to bind)

First make the pastry. Sift the flour and salt into a mixing bowl and make a well in the centre. Add the butter and rub it in lightly with your fingertips until the mixture looks like fine breadcrumbs. Add the water gradually, a tablespoon or 2 at a time, stirring it in with a spatula until the dough starts to come away from the sides of the bowl. Turn the dough on to a lightly floured board, gather it together and press it into a flat cake. Wrap in cling film and chill for 30 minutes.

Preheat the oven to 200°C/400°F/Gas Mark 6. Mix all the ingredients for the filling together in a bowl. On a floured board, roll out the pastry to about 5mm (¼ inch) thick and cut out 6 circles, about 18–20cm (7–8 inches) in diameter. Divide the filling between them, placing it on half of each circle. Brush the edges of the pastry with a little water, fold over and pinch together to seal. Place the pasties on a baking sheet and bake for 35 minutes, until golden brown.

Makes 6

BRAISED

PORK AND CLAMS WITH FRIED POTATOES

The Portuguese dish, *carne de porco a alentejana*, comes from the south coast but is a firm favourite throughout the whole country. This is an adaptation of the version I have enjoyed at my favourite south London café, O Cantina Portugal.

1kg (2^1/$_4$ pounds) pork neck fillet, cut into
   2cm (^{3}/$_4$ inch) pieces
4 garlic cloves, finely sliced
1 teaspoon sweet paprika
300ml (1^1/$_4$ cups) dry white wine
2 bay leaves
80ml (^{1}/$_3$ cup) olive oil
100g (^{1}/$_3$ cup) black olives
1kg (2^1/$_4$ pounds) clams
1 onion, finely chopped
1 tablespoon tomato purée
Sea salt and freshly ground black pepper

For the fried potatoes
200ml (scant 1 cup) vegetable oil
800g (1^3/$_4$ pounds) floury potatoes, peeled
   and cut into 1cm (^{1}/$_2$ inch) dice
Sweet paprika for dusting

In a large bowl, mix the pork with the garlic, paprika, wine and bay leaves, then cover and leave to marinate for 2–3 hours.

Drain the pork and reserve the marinade. Heat half the olive oil in a heavy-based pan, add the meat and season with salt and pepper. Fry over a medium heat for 8–10 minutes, until well browned, then stir in the marinade and the olives. Bring the mixture to the boil, reduce the heat to low and simmer for 30 minutes, until the pork is tender.

Meanwhile, wash the clams under cold running water to remove any grit or sand, discarding any open ones that don't close when tapped on the work surface. Heat the remaining olive oil in a separate pan, add the onion and cook until soft. Stir in the tomato purée, simmer for 5 minutes, then add the clams. Cover and cook for 4–5 minutes over a medium heat until all the clams are open, then add the mixture to the pork. Adjust the seasoning.

Heat the vegetable oil in a large frying pan, add the potato cubes and fry over a medium heat for about 12 minutes, until crisp and golden. Remove them with a slotted spoon and drain on kitchen paper. Sprinkle with sea salt and a little paprika.

Serve the pork and clams with the potatoes and maybe some lemon wedges on the side.

Serves 6

SALTFISH AND ACKEE

Cod is a coldwater fish and, in colonial times, the British used to barter salt cod from Newfoundland in the Caribbean in exchange for rum. The Caribbean islands have a great array of saltfish dishes, though this one is by far the most popular in the UK.

500g (1 pound 2 ounces) salt cod, soaked for 12 hours or overnight in several changes of water
50g (3$^1/_2$ tablespoons) unsalted butter
1 onion, finely sliced
1 garlic clove, sliced
1 green pepper, sliced
1 red pepper, sliced
1 red chilli, seeded and finely sliced
600g (1$^1/_4$ pounds) canned ackee, drained
3 ripe tomatoes, sliced into wedges
2 tablespoons chopped parsley
Sea salt and freshly ground black pepper
Sweet Potato Mash (see page 150), to serve

Drain the cod, put it in a saucepan and cover with fresh water. Bring to the boil, then reduce the heat and simmer gently for 15–20 minutes, until tender. Remove the fish from the water with a slotted spoon and drain well. When it is cool enough to handle, peel away the skin and bones and flake the flesh.

Melt the butter in a frying pan, add the onion, garlic, peppers and chilli and cook over a low heat until soft. Stir in the salt cod and parsley, then gently fold in the ackee. Add the tomatoes and season with pepper and maybe a little sea salt. Heat through and serve with the Sweet Potato Mash.

Serves 4

THAI RED FISH CURRY

I prefer the flavour of red curry with fish, as traditionally it uses coconut milk and is therefore not as harsh as a green curry. However, the flavour of this curry is still pretty powerful, so it is best to go for a robust fish, such as hake, skate or even swordfish.

You can make this curry as hot as you like. I use around 20g of paste for a medium-hot flavour. As with all curries, start with a little paste and add more to taste. You could make your own Thai curry paste but you can buy good authentic ones from Asian grocers. I like the Mae Ploy brand.

800g (1³/4 pounds) waxy potatoes, peeled and quartered
800ml (3¹/4 cups) coconut milk
20g (4 teaspoons) red curry paste, or to taste
1 teaspoon sugar
3 tablespoons Thai fish sauce
6 x 175g (6-ounce) fish steaks
Juice of 1 lime
A small bunch of coriander

Cook the potatoes in a pan of boiling water for 5 minutes to release the starch, then drain and set aside.

In a pan large enough to hold the fish in one layer, bring half the coconut milk to the boil. Add the curry paste and simmer for 3 minutes, until fragrant. Add the sugar and fish sauce and cook for a few minutes longer. Add the rest of the coconut milk and bring back to the boil, then put in the potatoes and simmer for 10 minutes or until they are almost cooked.

Add the fish and simmer gently for 3–5 minutes, until the fish and potatoes are done. Squeeze in the lime juice and check the flavour: add more fish sauce or sugar if it's needed. Strew with fresh coriander and serve with steamed rice.

Serves 6

TRINIDADIAN FISH CURRY

In the Caribbean this dish would usually be made with a whole fish such as a large red snapper. These are easy enough to come by here, though bream or even salmon steaks work perfectly, too. It is traditionally served with plantain, sweet potato or yams on the side, but I like to cook sweet potatoes in the sauce.

*1kg (2¼ pounds) snapper, or 2 x 500g
  (1 pound 2 ounce) black bream,
  or 4 salmon steaks*
½ teaspoon sea salt
*500g (1 pound 2 ounces) sweet potatoes,
  peeled and sliced*

For the marinade
1 large onion, sliced
3 garlic cloves, chopped
½ teaspoon turmeric
Juice of ½ lemon
Freshly ground black pepper

For the sauce
3 tablespoons vegetable oil
1 onion, chopped
2 garlic cloves, chopped
1 red chilli, seeded and chopped
4 teaspoons curry powder, preferably hot
3 tomatoes, chopped
*400ml (1⅔ cups) chicken stock (you can use
  a stock cube)*

If using whole fish, make 2 or 3 deep slashes to the bone with a sharp knife on each side of the fish. Rub the fish with the sea salt and place in a large baking dish while you make the marinade.

Put the marinade ingredients in a blender or food processor with about 2 tablespoons of water to get it going and blend to a smooth paste. Rub the paste all over the fish, inside the cavity and into the slashes, and leave to marinate for about 30 minutes.

Meanwhile, make the sauce. Pour the oil into a pan and warm it over a medium heat. When the oil is hot, add the onion, garlic and chilli and fry for 4–5 minutes, until they are soft and beginning to brown slightly. Add the curry powder and cook for 1 minute, then add the tomatoes and stock. Bring to the boil, reduce the heat to low and simmer for 30 minutes.

Preheat the oven to 180°C/350°F/Gas Mark 4. Scatter the sweet potatoes around the fish and pour over the curry sauce. Cover the dish with foil and bake for 30 minutes.

Serves 4

BRAISED CUTTLEFISH AND POTATOES

This recipe came to me courtesy of Jonathon Jones and Harry Lester, of the venerable Anchor and Hope in Waterloo, south London, and it's a dish I've enjoyed there many times. The cuttlefish absorbs the flavours of the fennel and Pernod, giving the stew a luscious Mediterranean accent. It's just the thing for a simple supper, with lots of crusty bread to mop up the juices.

1kg (2^1/$_4$ pounds) cuttlefish
130ml (^{1}/$_2$ cup) extra virgin olive oil
100ml (scant ^{1}/$_2$ cup) dry white wine
50ml (3^1/$_2$ tablespoons) Pernod
2 small fennel bulbs, finely sliced
4 garlic cloves, crushed
500g (1 pound 2 ounces) waxy new potatoes,
  peeled and cut into 2cm (^{3}/$_4$ inch) chunks
4 tomatoes, skinned and chopped
A 12cm- (5-inch-) long red chilli, slit open
  down the middle
A pinch of saffron threads
A small bunch of flat-leaf parsley, leaves
  roughly picked
1 red onion, finely sliced
Juice of ^{1}/$_2$ lemon
Sea salt and freshly ground black pepper

To clean the cuttlefish, cut along one side of the body, open it out flat and remove the cuttlebone. Pull the tentacles away and cut away the beak from the centre of the tentacles. Detach the ink sac, then remove and discard the guts. Wash the body and the tentacles under cold running water, then cut the body into 2cm (^{3}/$_4$ inch) squares. (You could ask your fishmonger to do all this.)

Preheat the oven to 160°C/325°F/Gas Mark 3. Place the diced cuttlefish and the tentacles in a casserole with 100ml (scant ^{1}/$_2$ cup) of the oil, plus the wine and Pernod. Massage the liquid into the cuttlefish, then add the fennel, garlic, potatoes and tomatoes. Put the casserole over a medium heat, bring slowly to the boil, then add the chilli and saffron. Season with salt and pepper, cover tightly and place in the oven. Cook for 1 hour, or until the cuttlefish is soft enough to cut with a spoon and the potatoes are on the verge of collapse.

Mix together the parsley and red onion and dress with the lemon juice and the remaining oil. To serve, ladle the cuttlefish into warmed bowls and top with the parsley and onion salad.

Serves 4

TUNA AND POTATO STEW

This typical Basque dish uses the belly of the tuna, along with the trio of peppers, potatoes and tomatoes that is so common in Spanish cooking. The belly is rich and more fatty than the loin, and is prized by the Japanese for sashimi, but it also braises very well. The loin can become a bit too dry when cooked in a sauce, so save that for the grill.

120ml (½ cup) olive oil
2 large onions, chopped
4 garlic cloves, chopped
1kg (2¼ pounds) waxy potatoes, peeled and
    cut into 2cm (¾ inch) chunks
500g (1 pound 2 ounces) tomatoes, skinned
    and chopped
4 red peppers, seeded and chopped
750g (1 pound 10 ounces) fresh tuna belly,
    skinned and cut into 2cm (¾ inch) chunks
2 tablespoons chopped parsley
Sea salt and freshly ground black pepper

Heat the olive oil in a large casserole, add the onions and garlic and cook over a low heat until soft and translucent. Add the potatoes, tomatoes and peppers, then cover and simmer for about 20 minutes. Put in the tuna, making sure it is completely covered; if not, add a little water. Season with salt and pepper. Cover and cook over a low heat for 15–20 minutes, until the tuna is tender. Sprinkle over the parsley and serve in deep bowls, with plenty of fresh crusty bread

Serves 6

GENOVESE SQUID AND POTATOES

Adapted from the great Marcella Hazan, this is a squid recipe I use all the time, almost to the point of exclusivity. Cuttlefish and octopus also enjoy this treatment at the Fox. I sometimes serve this on toast, or with pasta or polenta. I even mix it through salad leaves.

If you can get hold of the ink sac from the squid, add it at the same time as the tomatoes. It lends a rich sea flavour but can be frighteningly black.

1.2kg (2³/4 pounds) squid
200ml (scant 1 cup) extra virgin olive oil
6 garlic cloves, finely chopped
1¹/2 tablespoons chopped parsley
200ml (scant 1 cup) white wine
400g (14 ounces) tomatoes, skinned and
  chopped
500g (1 pound 2 ounces) waxy potatoes,
  peeled and cut into 4cm (1¹/2 inch) chunks
Sea salt and freshly ground black pepper

To clean the squid, hold the body in one hand and the tentacles in the other. Gently pull and twist and the head and tentacles will come away with the innards. Cut the tentacles away from the head and set aside. Squeeze out the hard beak, then cut it off and discard it.

Discard the head and innards. Pull away the purple membrane covering the squid, then remove the quill (which looks like a piece of transparent plastic) from inside the body. Wash the squid thoroughly under cold running water and drain. Cut it into rings. Put the oil in a large saucepan over a high heat until it is just smoking. Throw in the garlic and parsley, stirring all the time until the garlic becomes golden and nutty, then carefully put in the squid rings and tentacles. Using a long-handled spoon, stir the squid around in the garlicky oil; watch out, as it can spatter.

Pour in the wine and let it bubble for 2 minutes. Add the tomatoes, cover the pan and turn the heat down to a simmer. Cook for about 40 minutes, then add the potatoes. Season with salt and pepper, stir to coat the potatoes well and cover again. Cook slowly for about 20 minutes, until the potatoes are tender. Adjust the seasoning and serve immediately.

Serves 6

POTATO, PEA AND MONKFISH BHAJI

I was taught to cook this dish by my colleague at the Fox, Sathuee Pahlath. Sath is from Durban in South Africa, his family background is North Indian and he makes the most fabulous curries. This one is quick, easy and extremely delicious.

450g (1 pound) waxy potatoes, peeled and
   cut into 2cm ($^3/_4$ inch) chunks
4 tablespoons vegetable oil
$^1/_2$ teaspoon mustard seeds
$^1/_2$ teaspoon cumin seeds
$^1/_2$ teaspoon dried chilli flakes
800g (1$^3/_4$ pounds) monkfish fillet, cut into
   2cm ($^3/_4$ inch) chunks
$^1/_4$ teaspoon turmeric
1 teaspoon ground coriander
1 teaspoon sugar
250g (9 ounces) frozen peas, defrosted
1 teaspoon salt
3 tomatoes (about 400g/14 ounces in total),
   chopped
2 tablespoons chopped fresh coriander

Cook the potatoes in boiling salted water until almost tender, then drain and set aside. Pour the oil into a large frying pan and place it over a medium heat. When the oil is hot, throw in the mustard and cumin seeds and the chilli flakes. As soon as the mustard seeds begin to pop, add the fish. Stir-fry until the fish is sealed and browned all over. Now add the potatoes, turmeric, coriander and sugar and stir around. Put in the peas and stir again.

Add 250ml (1 cup) water and the salt. Bring to the boil, then cover, reduce the heat to low and simmer gently for 10 minutes. Add the tomatoes and simmer, uncovered, for 3 minutes. Scatter over the fresh coriander and serve with steamed rice.

Serves 4-6

OCTOPUS RECHADO

I was introduced to this dish at the Eagle by Tom Norrington-Davies, one of the many interesting recipes he brought back from his travels.

Rechado is a volatile curry paste from the south-western coast of India and would commonly be referred to in the UK as vindaloo. Brought to Goa by the Portuguese, it uses traditional European as well as Indian spices. In Goa the stew would usually be enriched with coconut milk but at the Eagle we brought it back to the Mediterranean with the addition of white wine. The rechado paste will keep, covered, in the fridge for 4 weeks. There should be plenty left to liven up any kind of fish, meat or poultry.

2 or 3 medium octopus, about 500g
  (1 pound 2 ounces) each
3 tablespoons olive oil
2 onions, chopped
3 red peppers, chopped
300ml (1^{1}/$_{4}$ cups) white wine
600g (1^{1}/$_{4}$ pounds) waxy potatoes, peeled
  and cut into 2cm (^{3}/$_{4}$ inch) chunks
1 teaspoon sugar
A bunch of coriander, chopped
Sea salt and freshly ground black pepper

For the rechado paste
1 teaspoon cumin seeds
2 tablespoons dried red chilli flakes
1 cinnamon stick, broken up
1 teaspoon cloves
1 teaspoon cardamom pods
2 tablespoons smoked paprika
3 bay leaves
1 tablespoon olive oil
1 onion, finely chopped
5 garlic cloves, finely chopped
1 teaspoon sea salt
100ml (scant ^{1}/$_{2}$ cup) white wine vinegar

First make the rechado. Heat a heavy-based frying pan, throw in all the spices and the bay leaves and dry-roast them over a low heat for about a minute, until they give off their aroma. Put the spices in a food processor and grind as finely as possible. Heat the oil in the same pan, add the onion and garlic and fry until softened. Add them to the ground spices with the salt and vinegar and blend to a smooth paste. If it's a little stiff, add some more oil.

To clean the octopus, use a sharp knife to cut the tentacles away from the head, just under the shell-like beak, and put them in a bowl of salted water. Rub them vigorously; the salt will help dislodge any sand caught in the suckers. Turn the body inside out, remove and discard all the internal organs and wash under cold running water. Slice the body into 2cm (^{3}/$_{4}$ inch) strips. (You could ask your fishmonger to do all this, if you prefer.)

Heat the oil in a large pan over a medium heat, add the onions and peppers and sauté until tender. Add the octopus, including the tentacles, and 2 tablespoons of the rechado paste. Turn up the heat and stir thoroughly. Add the wine and bring to the boil. Cover the pan, lower the heat and simmer gently for 1^{1}/$_{2}$ hours. Add the potatoes and a little water if needed to cover them. Cook for a further 20 minutes or until the potatoes are done and the octopus is tender.

Stir in the sugar and season with sea salt and pepper. Add more rechado if you want more heat. Scatter over the coriander and serve with steamed rice.

Serves 4

MOROCCAN FISH STEW

A simple but substantial stew from North Africa, where it would be cooked in a tagine – a traditional glazed earthenware dish with a conical lid. I don't have a tagine at home but I've made this successfully in a wide, lidded frying pan. The sauce, along with the potatoes and chick peas, can be cooked in advance and left for the flavours to mingle before adding the fish and the prawns.

50ml (3^1/$_2$ tablespoons) olive oil
2 onions, sliced
3 garlic cloves, sliced
1 teaspoon sweet paprika
1 teaspoon ground cumin
1 teaspoon harissa paste
1 red pepper, sliced into strips
400g (14 ounces) canned chopped tomatoes
1 tablespoon tomato purée
500g (1 pound 2 ounces) waxy potatoes,
  peeled and cut into 2cm (^{3}/$_4$ inch) chunks
700ml (2^3/$_4$ cups) fish stock
500g (1 pound 2 ounces) large raw prawns
400g (14 ounces) canned chick peas, drained
1kg (2^1/$_4$ pounds) white fish fillets, such as
  bass or bream, cut into slices 2cm
  (^{3}/$_4$ inch) thick
A small bunch of coriander
Sea salt and freshly ground black pepper

Heat the olive oil in a large pan, add the onions and garlic and sweat over a low heat until soft and translucent. Add the paprika and cumin, cook for 1 minute to take the harshness from the spices, then stir in the harissa, red pepper, canned tomatoes and tomato purée. Add the potatoes and pour in the fish stock. Bring to the boil, then turn the heat down to medium and simmer until the potatoes are just cooked.

Meanwhile, prepare the prawns. Pull the heads off the prawns, then peel off the shells, leaving on the tail shell. Use the tip of a sharp knife to remove the black intestinal vein from the back of each prawn. Wash the prawns and dry them well.

When the potatoes are done, add the chickpeas and return to the boil. Put in the fish pieces and the prawns. Simmer for 3–4 minutes, until the fish is done, then season with salt and pepper.

Serve in big warmed soup bowls, ladled over couscous and strewn with fresh coriander.

Serves 6

JUST POTATOES

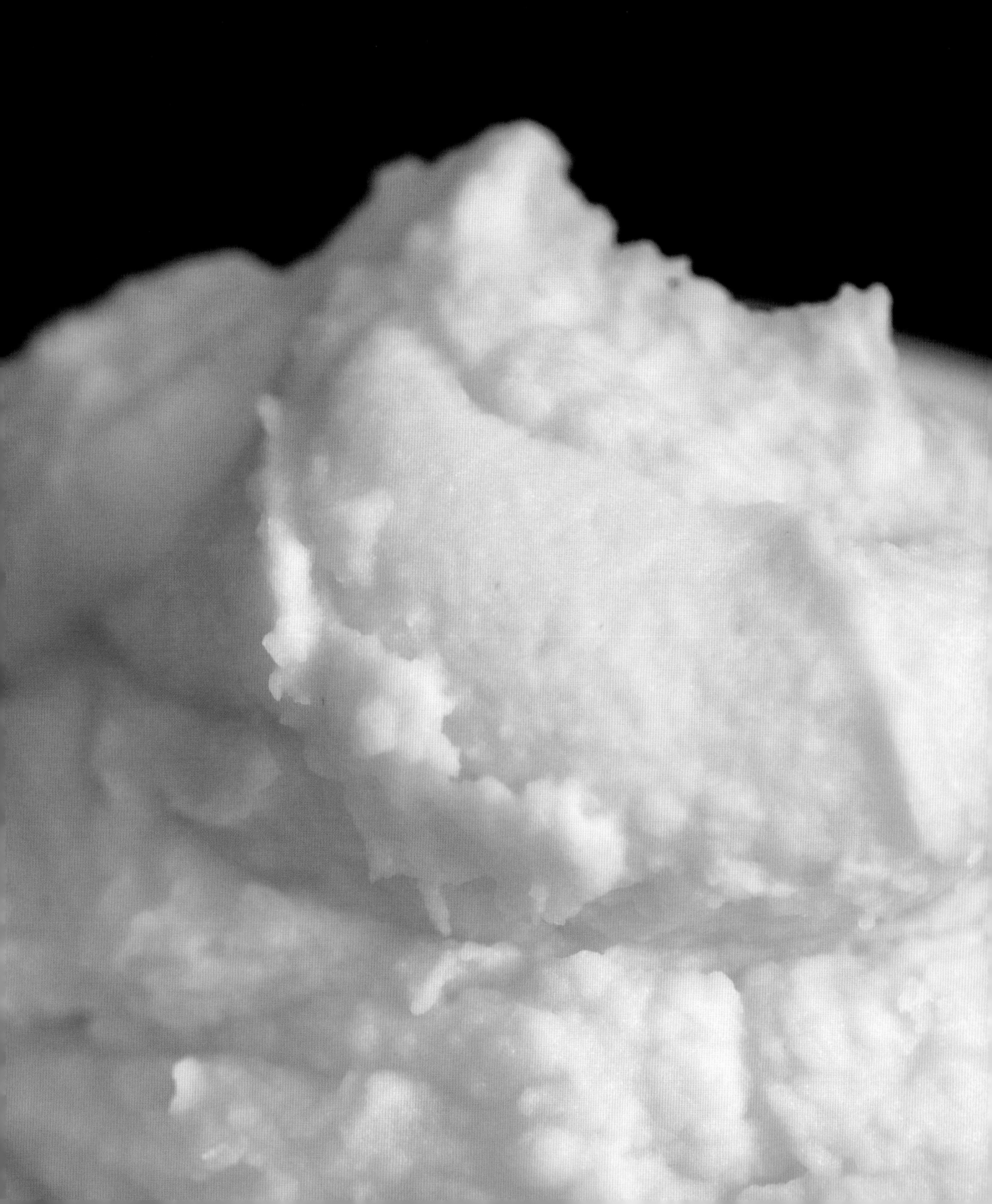

MASHED POTATO

The best potatoes for mash are the floury variety, though they are the most difficult to boil as they have a tendency to fall apart. One easy way is to boil the potatoes in their skins and peel them while they are still warm. Alternatively, put the potatoes in cold water, bring to the boil and simmer over a gentle heat so that they don't break apart and become waterlogged. The potatoes need to be drained very thoroughly and mashed with warm milk and melted butter – if they're warm they are easier to incorporate and won't cool the potatoes. And never mash potatoes in a food processor; the mash will be gluey.

1kg (2¼ pounds) floury potatoes
300ml (1¼ cups) milk
130g (½ cup) unsalted butter, plus extra to serve
Sea salt and freshly ground black pepper

If your potatoes are all roughly the same size, you can boil them whole in their skins; otherwise, peel them and cut them to an even size. Put them in a large pan, cover with plenty of cold water, add a good few pinches of sea salt and bring to the boil. Reduce the heat and simmer until tender. Drain well and return to the pan, then place over a low heat to evaporate the moisture. If using whole spuds, peel off the skins. Mash the potatoes with a potato masher or by putting them through a mouli-légumes or potato ricer.

In a small pan, warm the milk and butter together until the butter has melted. Pour about half the milk and butter into the potatoes and beat with a whisk or a wooden spoon until smooth. Adjust to your preferred consistency with the remaining milk mixture and season with salt and pepper. Serve with an extra lump of butter on top.

Serves 4

COLCANNON

Colcannon is not unlike bubble and squeak, although it is made with fresh vegetables rather than leftovers. Traditionally eaten in Ireland on Hallowe'en, the mash has a coin dropped into it and whoever receives it on their plate will have good luck for the year ahead. This makes a good accompaniment to roast cod or baked salmon.

1kg (2¼ pounds) floury potatoes
500g (1 pound 2 ounces) Savoy cabbage, sliced into strips
250ml (1 cup) milk
4 spring onions, finely sliced
100g (7 tablespoons) unsalted butter, plus extra to serve
Sea salt and freshly ground black pepper

Cook the potatoes as you would for mashed potatoes (see above), then drain and return to the pan. Meanwhile, steam the cabbage in a little salted water until tender, then drain thoroughly.

Warm the milk in a pan and add the spring onions. Simmer gently for 3 minutes, until the spring onions have softened slightly, then pour the mixture into the potatoes and mash together. Beat in the butter and fold in the cabbage. Season to taste and serve with an extra knob of butter on top.

Serves 4

CHAMP

Champ is another mashed potato dish eaten in Ireland, and also in Scotland. It should be served on individual plates with a crater dug into the top, which is filled with melted butter. Each forkful of mash is dipped into the pool.

1kg (2¼ pounds) floury potatoes
300ml (1¼ cups) milk
A bunch of spring onions, chopped
130g (½ cup) unsalted butter, plus extra to serve
Sea salt and freshly ground black pepper

Cook the potatoes as you would for mashed potatoes (see above), then drain and return to the pan. Warm the milk in a pan and add the spring onions. Simmer gently for 3 minutes, until the spring onions have softened slightly, then pour the mixture into the potatoes and mash together with the butter. Season to taste.

Divide the mash between warmed serving plates and make a well in the centre of each portion. Add as much diced butter as you wish to the craters; it should melt from the heat of the potatoes. Dip each forkful of mash into the melted butter as you eat.

Serves 4

HASSELBACK POTATOES

Originating from Joseph Hasselback's Stockholm restaurant, these 'hedgehog-style' garlicky roast potatoes are fantastic alongside a big, robust roast fish, such as wild salmon or turbot. It's essential not to cut right through the potatoes; they should fan out into a distinctive shape. A skewer will help hold each potato together as you cut it.

1kg (2¼ pounds) medium-sized waxy potatoes, peeled
100g (7 tablespoons) unsalted butter
50ml (3½ tablespoons) olive oil
12 garlic cloves, peeled and lightly crushed with the back of a knife
6 fresh bay leaves
Sea salt and freshly ground black pepper

Preheat the oven to 190°C/375°F/Gas Mark 5. Spear each potato with a skewer about 5mm (¼ inch) from the base, then hold tightly and carefully slice the potato at 5mm (¼ inch) intervals with a sharp knife, cutting down only as far as the skewer. Remove the skewers and carefully rinse the potatoes under cold running water to remove the starch. This should stop the potato slices sticking back together while cooking.

Melt the butter and olive oil in a roasting dish. Stir in the garlic cloves and add the potatoes in a single layer, being careful not to break them. Season with salt and pepper, tear the bay leaves in half and add them to the dish. Put the dish in the oven and roast for 25–30 minutes, basting occasionally with the butter and oil, until the potatoes are golden brown and have opened up like a fan.

Serves 4

STEAMED NEW POTATOES COOKED IN PARCELS

Perfect for the finest new potatoes – the first Jersey Royals are best. The flavour of the dill should be completely absorbed by the potatoes. They are best served with a simple poached fish.

900g (2 pounds) small new potatoes
75g (⅓ cup) unsalted butter, melted
6 sprigs of dill
Sea salt and freshly ground black pepper

Preheat the oven to 200°C/400°F/Gas Mark 6. Cut out 6 circles of baking parchment, about 24cm (10 inches) in diameter.

Wash and dry the potatoes and roll them in the melted butter. Divide the potatoes between the paper circles, placing them to one side of the paper. Season with salt and pepper, top with a sprig of dill, then fold over the paper and roll over the edges a couple of times to seal. Put the parcels on a baking sheet and cook for 25–30 minutes. The paper will brown and puff up. Serve immediately in the parcels, which should be opened at the table so people can savour the aroma.

Serves 6

CRUSHED NEW POTATOES

A simple dish to complement roast or grilled fish.

750g (1 pound 10 ounces) waxy new potatoes, scraped
75ml (5 tablespoons) extra virgin olive oil
A splash of balsamic vinegar, to taste
50g (2 ounces) mixed parsley, tarragon and basil, roughly chopped
Sea salt and freshly ground black pepper

Cook the potatoes in plenty of boiling salted water until tender. Drain them well and return to the pan. Pour in the olive oil and crush the potatoes lightly with a fork until they break apart. Season with salt, pepper and a splash of balsamic vinegar. Gently fold in the chopped herbs and serve immediately.

Serves 4

POTATO GNOCCHI

Gnocchi make regular appearances on the menu at the Fox. These light and silky potato dumplings are as popular served as a simple vegetarian main course as they are in a fishy broth (see page 18) or tossed in a rich tomato and anchovy sauce (see page 156).

500g (1 pound 2 ounces) floury potatoes
150g (scant 3/4 cup) fine semolina
Sea salt and freshly ground black pepper

Put the potatoes, in their skins, in a pan of salted water and bring to the boil. Reduce the heat and simmer until tender, then drain. Peel them while they are still a little warm, then return to the pan and mash them.

Turn the mashed potato out on to a board and sprinkle with salt and pepper; it will be more easily absorbed at this point. Make a well in the centre of the potato, add the semolina and quickly work the mixture into a firm dough. If necessary, add a little extra semolina until the dough is firm and no longer sticky.

Preheat the oven to 140°C/275°F/Gas Mark 1 and lightly oil a gratin dish. Bring a large pot of water to the boil.

Divide the potato mixture into 4, roll each piece into a long sausage and cut into 1cm (1/2 inch) lengths. Traditionally each piece is rolled over the tines of a fork to make distinctive ridges for the sauce to cling to. Poach the gnocchi by dropping them into the boiling water in batches and, as they rise to the surface, simmering for about 1 minute.

Remove the dumplings from the pan with a slotted spoon, drain and transfer to the gratin dish. Keep warm in the oven until you have finished cooking all the gnocchi. Then either pour over a sauce or drop them into your soup. Serve at once.

Serves 4–6

CHIPS

A warning note on chips. Domestic kitchens are not really set up for chip frying unless you have a deep-fat fryer. The best chips are cooked twice – first on a low heat to cook the flesh through and then on a high heat to crisp the outside – so the oil needs to be thermostatically controlled. There should be plenty of oil, so you can move the potatoes around easily and they cook evenly. Never overcrowd the pan, or the heat will be reduced and the potatoes will boil rather than fry and absorb too much oil. Instead, cook the chips in batches. Keep them warm in a low oven while you fry more – and there will be more because everybody loves chips.

1kg (2 1/4 pounds) floury potatoes
Vegetable or sunflower oil for deep-frying
Sea salt and freshly ground black pepper

Peel the potatoes and cut them into long strips 1cm (1/2 inch) thick. Rinse well under cold running water to remove the starch, then dry on a tea towel.

Heat the oil to 130°C/260°F in a deep-fat fryer. Place a single layer of chips in the basket and lower it into the oil. Fry for about 5 minutes, until tender right through but still pale. Lift the chips out in the frying basket, drain off the excess oil and turn them on to kitchen paper. Repeat with the rest of the potatoes. At this point the blanched chips will hold nicely and you can continue with the second frying just before you need them.

Raise the oil temperature to 190°C/375°F and cook the chips, again in batches, for about 2 minutes, until they are golden and crisp. Sprinkle with sea salt and pepper and serve at once.

Serves 4

VARIATION: THIN CHIPS

If you require thinner chips, to sit alongside steamed mussels or fishcakes perhaps, cut the potatoes into 5mm (1/4 inch) strips and then continue as above. The initial blanching should take only about 3 minutes and the final frying 1–2 minutes.

POTATO SCALLOPS

Steaming hot, salty and vinegary, these were always my chip-shop favourite. They made a great after-school treat for impoverished students, as we could buy just one or two at a time – plus they were much cheaper than a bag of chips and had the added appeal of the crisp batter.

3 large floury potatoes, weighing about 600g
  (1¹/₄ pounds) in total
Vegetable oil for deep-frying
1 quantity of Beer Batter (see page 84)
Sea salt

Peel the potatoes and slice them as thinly as you can. Wash the slices under cold running water and pat dry with a tea towel.

Heat some oil in a deep-fat fryer to 180°C/350°F. Dip a few slices of potato into the batter, shake off the excess and drop them into the hot oil. Fry in batches until the scallops begin to float and are golden and crisp. Drain on kitchen paper and sprinkle with salt immediately, so that it sticks. Keep warm in a low oven while you cook the rest. Serve with vinegar, tomato ketchup, or mayonnaise or any sauce you like.

Serves 6

BARBECUED BAKED POTATOES

This is one of my favourite recipes for baked potatoes. The flames of the barbecue penetrate the flesh, giving it a wonderful smoky flavour. It takes a little time, as do most baked potatoes, but you can speed up the process, if you like, by parboiling the potatoes first.

Baking potatoes
Olive oil
Sea salt

Wash the potatoes and pat them dry. Stab each potato about 5 or 6 times with a fork, rub with olive oil and sprinkle with sea salt. Place the potatoes directly on the grill over the hot coals and cook for about 1 hour, until a skewer inserted into the centre goes in easily.

SWEET POTATO CRISPS

The sweet potato is a native of Latin America, discovered in Haiti and brought back to Europe by Christopher Columbus. It is also a staple of Jamaica, the southern states of America and Polynesia. Sweet potatoes can be baked or mashed but they also make great crisps. Serve with grilled fish.

2–3 sweet potatoes
Vegetable oil for deep-frying
Sea salt and freshly ground black pepper

Peel the sweet potatoes and cut them into wafer-thin slices – the easiest way to do this is with a vegetable peeler. Heat the oil to 160°C/325°F in a deep-fat fryer and fry the slices, in batches, for 2–3 minutes, until crisp. Drain on kitchen paper, season with salt and pepper and serve immediately.

Serves 4

**Ways with potato –
clockwise from top-left:**
Mash, Hasselback, Sweet Potato Crisps,
Steamed New Potatoes

SWEET POTATO MASH

This makes a lovely accompaniment to Ceviche (see page 46) or grilled fish. I usually serve this mash at room temperature, though it is just as good warm. Sometimes I add a little chopped red chilli at the end to liven it up, then finish it off with a splash of fruity olive oil.

500g (1 pound 2 ounces) sweet potatoes
Juice of 1 lime
2 tablespoons extra virgin olive oil
A small bunch of coriander, chopped
Sea salt and freshly ground black pepper

Preheat the oven to 180°C/350°F/Gas Mark 4. Put the sweet potatoes on a baking sheet and bake for 30–40 minutes, until tender. Remove and leave until cool enough to handle, then split them open and scoop out the flesh into a bowl. Mash with a fork and add the lime juice, olive oil and chopped coriander. Season with salt and pepper to taste.

Serves 4

SWEET POTATOES IN COCONUT MILK

This dish is Polynesian in origin. Most of the vegetables eaten in those islands tend to be starchy and are stewed or mashed, then served with rice alongside grilled fish. Ordinary potatoes or pumpkin can be substituted for the sweet potato and unripe bananas for the plantain.

700g (1¹/₂ pounds) sweet potatoes, peeled and diced
1 onion, finely diced
400ml (1²/₃ cups) coconut milk
2 plantains, peeled and sliced
Sea salt

Put the sweet potatoes, onion and a pinch of salt in a saucepan and cover with the coconut milk, adding a little water if needed. Bring to the boil, then turn the heat down low and simmer for

10 minutes. Add the plantains and cook for a further 10–15 minutes, until the vegetables are soft.

Serves 4

SWEET POTATO CORNBREAD

A cross between a cake and bread, this is eaten throughout the Deep South of America and the Caribbean. I serve it as an accompaniment to dishes such as Saltfish and Ackee (see page 133), or to go alongside Ceviche (see page 46).

500g (1 pound 2 ounces) sweet potatoes
50g (3¹/₂ tablespoons) unsalted butter, plus extra
  for greasing the tin
2 free-range eggs, lightly beaten
¹/₂ teaspoon bicarbonate of soda
1 teaspoon sea salt
30g (2 tablespoons) brown sugar
125g (¹/₂ cup) plain yoghurt
250g (1²/₃ cups) polenta

Preheat the oven to 180°C/Gas Mark 4. Liberally butter a large loaf tin. Bake the sweet potatoes in their skins until they are tender. Leave until cool enough to handle, then split them open and scoop out the flesh. Purée the flesh in a food processor with the butter, eggs, bicarbonate of soda, salt and sugar until smooth, then fold in the yoghurt and polenta. Pour into the prepared tin and bake for 20 minutes, or until golden brown and bouncy to the touch.

Serves 6

MAYONNAISE

Mayonnaise is a most versatile sauce. It can be enriched with garlic, freshened with herbs or made piquant with gherkins and capers. Your basic mayo should be made with a neutral unsaturated oil, such as sunflower or vegetable; olive oil is too strong and can taste bitter. You can make mayonnaise by hand but this is a speedy food-processor version.

3 free-range egg yolks
1 tablespoon Dijon mustard
1 tablespoon lemon juice
350ml (1¹/₂ cups) sunflower or vegetable oil
Sea salt and freshly ground black pepper

Blend the egg yolks, mustard and lemon juice together in a food processor until well combined. With the machine running, gradually add the oil in a thin, steady stream until you have incorporated it all. If it is too thick, add a little warm water to thin it down. Season with salt and pepper and adjust the acidity with a little more lemon juice to taste.

VARIATION:
TARTARE SAUCE
Make the mayonnaise as above, then stir in 1 tablespoon chopped capers, 1 tablespoon chopped gherkin, 1 small shallot, finely chopped, 1 tablespoon chopped parsley, 1 teaspoon chopped tarragon and 1 hard-boiled egg, grated. This sauce is the ultimate partner for fish and chips.

VARIATION:
MARIE ROSE SAUCE
The classic prawn cocktail sauce. Make the mayonnaise as above, then stir in 2 tablespoons tomato ketchup, 1 teaspoon Worcestershire sauce, a few drops of Tabasco sauce and a squeeze of lemon juice.

AIOLI

Aioli is a strong, garlicky mayonnaise eaten in the south of France with poached fish and vegetables. In Provence, there is a dish known as *le grand aioli*, which is eaten to mark important occasions. It contains poached salt cod or fresh fish, boiled potatoes, carrots, peppers, beetroot, artichokes, asparagus, chick peas, green beans, hard-boiled eggs, sometimes whelks, winkles, sea snails or octopus – and, of course, lashings of aioli. In France only olive oil would be used in this sauce but I cut it with half vegetable oil so it's not too bitter.

3 free-range egg yolks
1 tablespoon Dijon mustard
6 garlic cloves, chopped
Juice of ¹/₂ lemon
200ml (scant 1 cup) vegetable oil
200ml (scant 1 cup) olive oil
Sea salt and freshly ground black pepper

Blend the egg yolks, mustard, garlic and lemon juice together in a food processor. Then add the oils gradually in a slow, steady stream, just like mayonnaise. Season with salt and pepper, then add a little more lemon juice if you like a sharper flavour.

ROUILLE

A rich, fiery-red accompaniment to fish soups and bouillabaisse in France. I also like to serve it with grilled or barbecued fish.

12 saffron threads
3 free-range egg yolks
3 garlic cloves, chopped
1 tablespoon Dijon mustard
1 red chilli, chopped
350ml (1¹/₂ cups) olive oil
1 teaspoon tomato purée
Sea salt and freshly ground black pepper

Pour 1 tablespoon of boiling water over the saffron and leave to steep for 5 minutes. In a food processor, blend the egg yolks, garlic, mustard and chilli to a smooth paste. Gradually add the olive oil in a thin, steady stream until it is all incorporated. Mix in the tomato purée and the saffron liquid, then season with salt and pepper. Rouille should be easily spoonable, so if it is too thick just let it down with a little warm water.

SALSA VERDE

A piquant green sauce to serve alongside grilled or poached fish, or simply toss with hot new potatoes for a wonderful warm salad.

1 shallot, chopped
80g (¹/₂ cup) capers, well drained
1 garlic clove, chopped
6 anchovy fillets
1 tablespoon Dijon mustard
A large bunch of flat-leaf parsley, roughly chopped
3 sprigs of tarragon, roughly chopped
350ml (1¹/₂ cups) extra virgin olive oil
1 tablespoon lemon juice
Sea salt and freshly ground black pepper

Blend together, or pound in a pestle and mortar, the shallot, capers, garlic and anchovies to make a thick paste. Beat in the mustard, chopped herbs and olive oil. Season with salt and pepper and the lemon juice. Use the salsa within 24 hours, as it loses its colour and texture fairly quickly.

ANCHOIADE

This recipe makes a fairly large batch of fantastic anchovy dressing but don't worry – it's so moreish you'll find yourself eating it on toast. Makes a particularly good Caesar dressing, too.

150g (5 ounces) anchovies in oil, drained
2 garlic cloves, chopped
2 teaspoons Dijon mustard
1 tablespoon sherry vinegar
350ml (1¹/₂ cups) extra virgin olive oil
1 small red chilli, chopped
1 teaspoon fresh thyme, or basil in summer
Freshly ground black pepper

Purée the anchovies, garlic, mustard and vinegar in a food processor until you have a smooth paste. With the machine running, slowly add the olive oil in a thin, steady stream, as if you were making mayonnaise. Season with pepper and then pulse in the chilli and herbs.

CHERMOULA

This spicy, aromatic paste from North Africa can be used as a marinade for fish or shellfish before grilling them on the barbecue, or in the base of a fish stew with the addition of wine and tomatoes.

4 garlic cloves, chopped
1 teaspoon ground cumin
1 teaspoon ground coriander
1 teaspoon sweet paprika
1 red chilli, seeded and chopped
A pinch of saffron threads
A small bunch of coriander
Juice of 1 lemon
5–6 tablespoons extra virgin olive oil
1 teaspoon sea salt

Blend all the ingredients together in a food processor to create a thick paste. The chermoula will keep in an airtight container in the fridge for up to 4 weeks.

HOLLANDAISE SAUCE

Hollandaise sauce is a traditional partner to poached salmon or trout but it also sits beautifully alongside more robust white fish, such as halibut or turbot. I use this rich, eggy sauce as a dip for steamed asparagus and artichokes, too.

200g (scant 1 cup) unsalted butter
50ml (3¹/₂ tablespoons) white wine vinegar
2 tablespoons water
3 free-range egg yolks
Juice of ¹/₂ lemon
Sea salt and freshly ground black pepper

Gently melt the butter and then leave it to cool a little. Put the vinegar and water into a small pan over a medium heat and simmer until reduced to 1 tablespoon.

Pour this reduction into a mixing bowl that will fit comfortably over a saucepan half filled with hot water, making sure the water doesn't touch the base of the bowl. Place the pan over a medium heat. Add the egg yolks to the bowl and whisk with a balloon whisk until thick and foamy. Gradually add the melted butter, whisking constantly until all of it has been incorporated. You should have a thick, creamy sauce. Season with sea salt, pepper and lemon juice to taste, then serve straight away.

BEARNAISE SAUCE

This is most often eaten with steak and chips. However, the aniseed bite of the tarragon also goes beautifully with grilled fish and, of course, chips.

200g (scant 1 cup) unsalted butter
50ml (3¹/₂ tablespoons) white wine vinegar
1 shallot, finely chopped
2 tablespoons water
1 tablespoon chopped tarragon (keep the stalks)
3 free-range egg yolks
Lemon juice to taste
Sea salt and freshly ground black pepper

Gently melt the butter and then allow it to cool a little. Put the vinegar, shallot, water and the stalks from the tarragon in a small pan over a low heat. Bring to the boil and simmer until reduced to 1 tablespoon of liquid. Strain the liquid into a mixing bowl that will fit comfortably over a saucepan half filled with hot water, making sure the water doesn't touch the base of the bowl. Now place the pan over a medium heat. Add the egg yolks to the bowl and whisk with a balloon whisk until thick and foamy. Gradually add the melted butter, whisking constantly until all of it has been incorporated. You should have a thick, creamy sauce. Season with sea salt, pepper and lemon juice to taste, then stir in the chopped tarragon. Serve straight away.

PIRI PIRI

Piri piri is a ferocious Portuguese marinade used to baste fish, prawns and, best of all, squid before grilling them on a barbecue. In Portugal, it is made using the small red chillies of the same name. I was introduced to piri piri by David Eyre when I was working at the Eagle. This is an adaptation of his recipe. Make it as hot or as mild as you like.

2 red peppers
6 or more red chillies, seeded
2 garlic cloves, peeled
3 bay leaves
2 teaspoons ground coriander
2 teaspoons sea salt
3 tablespoons wine vinegar
About 200ml (scant 1 cup) olive oil

Grill the red peppers all over until the skin has blackened, then leave to cool a little. When cool enough to handle, peel and seed them. Put the peppers in a food processor and blend with all the remaining ingredients except the oil. Gradually mix in enough oil to make a loose paste. Taste to check the heat, adding more chilli if necessary.

**A spin on mayonnaise –
clockwise from top-left:**
Mayonnaise, Tartare sauce, Aioli,
Marie Rose Sauce

SKORDALIA

In Greece, this cold garlic and potato sauce is served with salted, poached or grilled fish and also with vegetables. Use as much or as little garlic as you want, though I usually make a pretty powerful version.

*3 small floury potatoes, weighing about 300g
   (11 ounces) in total
About 6 garlic cloves, peeled
200ml (scant 1 cup) extra virgin olive oil
Juice of 1 lemon
50ml (3$\frac{1}{2}$ tablespoons) milk
Sea salt and freshly ground black pepper*

Cook the potatoes in their skins in boiling salted water until tender, then drain. When they are cool enough to handle, peel and mash them. Crush the garlic to a paste with a pinch of salt in a mortar and pestle or in a bowl. Mix the potato and garlic together, then gradually add the oil and lemon juice alternately with the milk, to taste. The sauce should have the consistency of mayonnaise; if it is too thick, let it down with a few more drops of milk. Season with salt and pepper.

TOMATO AND ANCHOVY SAUCE

This quick and simple tomato sauce suits potato gnocchi perfectly, and also makes a good accompaniment to grilled or roast fish. Frying the garlic until it is golden and fragrant gives the sauce a nutty flavour and is known as *aglio d'oro*, or golden garlic.

*50ml (3$\frac{1}{2}$ tablespoons) olive oil
2 garlic cloves, finely chopped
400g (14 ounces) tomatoes, skinned and chopped,
   or canned tomatoes, drained
50g (2 ounces) anchovies in oil, drained
Sea salt and freshly ground black pepper*

Heat the olive oil in a heavy-based pan until it is almost smoking, then add the garlic. Stir constantly and, just as the garlic is turning golden, pour in the tomatoes. Simmer the sauce on the lowest possible heat for 20–25 minutes; when it is ready, the oil will separate from the tomatoes and float to the top. Chop the anchovies and stir through the sauce. Season with salt and pepper.

MUSHY PEAS 1

Mushy peas are an essential accompaniment to fish and chips. They should really be made the traditional way with dried marrowfat peas but I can never resist sweet fresh peas in spring, so I'm giving two recipes – the classic version here and a lighter one made with fresh peas below.

*250g (9 ounces) dried marrowfat peas
1 teaspoon bicarbonate soda
40g (3 tablespoons) unsalted butter
Sea salt and freshly ground black pepper*

Put the marrowfat peas in a bowl, cover with at least 4 times their volume of water and add the bicarbonate of soda. Leave to soak for at least 4 hours, preferably overnight.

Drain the peas and rinse them. Put them in a pan, cover with fresh water and bring to the boil. Reduce the heat to a simmer, skimming off any frothy scum from the surface, and cook for 1–1$\frac{1}{2}$ hours, until the peas are soft. Drain off any liquid left in the pan and beat in the butter. Season with salt and pepper.

MUSHY PEAS 2

*A sprig of mint
250g (9 ounces) fresh podded peas
40g (3 tablespoons) unsalted butter
Sea salt and freshly ground black pepper*

Bring a pot of lightly salted water to the boil with the sprig of mint. Drop in the peas and boil for 5 minutes or until they are tender and sweet. Drain, pull out the mint and mash the peas with the butter. Season with salt and pepper.

INDEX